CW00420560

John Hawley was a Dartmouth merchant who became a privateer admiral and was the scourge of the Bretons during the middle part of the Hundred Years War. He effectively ran Dartmouth for nearly forty years, serving as its mayor fourteen times and representing it in Parliament for four terms. He became a public hero and yet was for a time imprisoned in the Tower of London.

He almost certainly met Geoffrey Chaucer, of whom he was a close contemporary, and was probably the object of the satirical portrait of the rascally Shipman in *The Canterbury Tales*.

Dartmouth occupied an important place in the life of the English nation during Hawley's lifetime, its shifting population confronting war and pestilence with a dogged resilience, led by a group of confident oligarchs of which John Hawley was the undisputed and charismatic leader. He lived his whole life in a time of war, albeit one punctuated by edgy and often unreliable truces. He shone brightly at that time and in that place because a combination of political, economic, and other factors created unique challenges and opportunities to which he responded with a brilliant energy.

This is the story of a terrible time, an exciting place and an extraordinary man.

Michael Connors was born in the ancient demesne of Townstal, Dartmouth in 1949. He learned to read and write less than a hundred yards from the site of John Hawley's house and to sail in the waters once plied by Hawley's cogs. After reading economic history as an undergraduate and completing a doctorate in Japanese studies, he embarked on a career in international finance, living in Japan for fifteen years. He and his family now divide their time between London and Dartmouth, and are sometimes to be seen walking their dogs near the remains of Hawley's fortalice.

The Latin inscription below the Hawley brass at St. Saviour's Church, Dartmouth (see above) reads, when translated, as follows:

Here lies a worthy man, John Hauley, builder of the chancel, who died on the 30th day of December in the year of Our Lord 1408; on the right lies his first wife by name Joan who died on the 12th day of July in the year of Our Lord 1394; on the left lies his second wife by name Alice who died on the 7th day of January in the year of Our Lord 1403; on whose souls may God have mercy, Amen.

Chaucer's Shipman of Dartmouth

John Hawley

Merchant, Mayor and Privateer

Michael Connors

"Blow the wind high, blow the wind low,
It always blows fair to Hawley's Hoe."

Richard
Webb

Dedication

For my friend Ron Gould

An American gentleman and adoptive Dartmothian

First published in the United Kingdom in 2008 by Richard Webb, Publisher

Text © 2008 Michael Connors
Maps © 2008 Nick Shillabeer
Design and typography © 2008 Richard Webb, Publisher

Michael Connors has asserted his right to be identified as the author of this work.

This book is sold subject to the condition that it shall not, by way of trade
or otherwise circulated without the publisher's prior consent in any form of binding
or cover other than that in which it is published and without a similar condition
including this condition being imposed on the subsequent purchaser

Designed by Laurence Daeche, Anon Design Co., Christchurch, Dorset

A CIP catalogue record for this book is available from the British Library

ISBN 978-0-9536361-8-1

Typesetting: Titling: Blackmoor. Body copy: 10/13pt Adobe Caslon

• 168 pages including 8 in colour plus colour endpapers
• 70 illustrations including 21 in colour and 5 maps • hardback • 73,000 words and a
comprehensive index • seven chapters and extensive notes, timeline and bibliography

Printed and bound in the United Kingdom by Short Run Press, Exeter, Devon

Richard Webb, Publisher
Dartmouth, Devon, England

www.dartmouthbooks.co.uk

Foreword

A salty, gnarled hand grips the forestay, a brown weather beaten face, matching his leather jerkin, scans forward. A shout from the towering fortalice and he glances to his left and waves back, a distant sound of church bells makes him look up river where a gathering of townsfolk are waving and pointing at his approach. Towing behind him, on a ragged rope, wallows another vessel flying a foreign pennant.

This is a romantic image of our 14th century local hero, standing at the prow of his ship, the *Christopher*, as she sails into the Dart on a flooding tide towing a captured vessel.

But who was the real John Hawley? He was the owner of this ship and many others, a privateer, admiral, mayor, MP and collector of customs, landowner, merchant trader, builder of Dartmouth's fortalice and benefactor of St Saviour's chancel.

Michael Connors has written a fascinating book about this early adventurer who lived during an emerging and troubled time for both Dartmouth and England. His meticulous research and attention to detail has resulted in a scholarly account of the life of this energetic 14th century character.

A character of whom Dartmouth can be justly proud.

Sir Geoffrey Newman

Publisher's Note:

The Newman family have since 1796 owned land around Blackpool, where a local militia force under the command of John Hawley defeated a formidable Breton invasion in April 1404. Their connections with the River Dart as merchant venturers and ship owners stretch back to 1442, only six years after John Hawley's son, John Hawley the Younger, died. There is therefore a virtually unbroken timeline between these two distinguished Dartmouth families: the Newman family of today and the Hawleys of the 14th and 15th centuries.

Contents

Author's Note

On a sunny September morning in 1954, I jumped off the rear platform of a green double-decker bus in Lower Street in Dartmouth and clambered up the flight of granite steps which took me up to Newcomen Road, and thence to my first day at school. In so doing, I unwittingly passed through the space where had stood, until a century or so earlier, the ancient Guildhall which was originally the residence of John Hawley.

When I was a child, we bought our stamps at the Post Office in Hauley Road and, then as now, all the Lower Ferry tugs bore the name Hauley – although I for years assumed that this latter naming was intended as some kind of pun. Like most Dartmothians, I have been vaguely aware of the Hawley legend since my childhood but the stimulus for the more detailed investigation which led to this book came from my reading the accounts of his life in the late Percy Russell's *Dartmouth* (1950) and Ray Freeman's *Dartmouth and its Neighbours.* (1990/updated 2007)

Primary sources for those who would delve into the times when John Hawley lived are invariably written in archaic hands and in Middle English, Norman French or Medieval Latin and, as such, are doubly inaccessible to the non-professional. We are therefore heavily dependent on the work of others. Unquestionably my most valuable printed source has been Hugh R. Watkin's 1935 compilation, *Dartmouth Pre-Reformation*, published under the imprint of the Devonshire Association. In the introduction to this work, Watkin in turn gives credit to a Mr. Stuart A. Moore F.S.A. who in 1879-80 carefully examined and indexed the extraordinarily large collection of documents, dating from 1286, that had been retained and were, at that time, stored in the town gaol opposite St Saviour's church. When using transcripts and translations of this kind of material, and standard reference works such as Roskell, Clark and Rawcliffe's magnificent *The House of Commons 1386 -1421*, on which I have drawn extensively for details of Hawley's activities as an MP, we are benefiting from works of monumental scholarship to which, as Beethoven said of Handel, we can but bend the knee.

As regards electronic media, I have refrained from giving detailed attributions in some cases, for fear that the changing world of the internet would soon render the references meaningless, but have referred to many such sources. Especially valuable has been the full, digitised version of the *Calendar of Patent Rolls* to which the University of Iowa has kindly given free online access. The National Archive's CD ROM version of the *Parliament Rolls of Medieval England* also warrants particular mention, while I have made frequent use of sources such as Wikipedia – to identify saints' days or remind myself quickly on matters such as the order of Capetian succession – and Google Earth, better to understand the geography of some of the actions in which Hawley and his men engaged.

Medieval spelling was notoriously inconsistent. Watkin's index lists fourteen different spellings of Hawley's surname alone, viz. Hawle, Hauley, Hawlee, Haulegh, Hawlegh, Haulee, Hawelegh, Hawley, Hauleygh, Haulech, Haweley, Hawele, de Hawlee and Howly. Where quoting directly from transcripts, I have rendered whichever version appears in the original, whilst elsewhere using 'Hawley', which modern historians have adopted as standard and is the most common spelling of the family's name today. All quotations feature the original, or transcribed, spellings but, in the main body of the text, I have used the modern standard British spellings for words of all kinds.

I would like to thank Richard Webb and Jess and Elly Connors for their editorial input and Ray Freeman for her support and her valuable comments on the manuscript. The remaining faults in and weaknesses of this work are, of course, entirely my responsibility.

This book is being published in the year which marks the six-hundredth anniversary of John Hawley's death, in the hope that it will help to keep his memory alive. I have endeavoured to relay the recorded facts accurately and to draw inferences and make extrapolations which are logical and reasonable, whilst accepting that these processes inevitably often involve a substantial element of speculation and are open to alternative interpretations. I hope that the professional medievalist will not find too much which is objectionable herein but, if any should do so and thus be provoked into writing a more scholarly and complete biography of this extraordinary and colourful man, I would be more than content. I submit that John Hawley's story is one which is well worth the telling – and believe that Geoffrey Chaucer, in his characteristic, tongue-in-cheek fashion, thought so too.

Michael Connors **Southtown, Dartmouth**
June 2008

Introduction

"A Schipman was ther…"

In the east aisle of the south transept of Westminster Abbey, can be found the tomb of Geoffrey Chaucer. Chaucer died, in a house that he had leased in the precincts of the Abbey, on October 25th 1400 and was interred nearby. His remains were later moved to their current resting place which, famous as Poets' Corner, attracts visitors from all over the world.

One hundred and seventy miles to the south-west as the crow flies, on the floor of the chancel, between the altar and the magnificent rood screen of St Saviour's Church in Dartmouth, lies a rectangle of cheap domestic carpet which gives makeshift protection to one of that church's treasures – an elaborate brass engraving that marks the grave of a man who was buried there early in the New Year of 1409. The brass portrays a knightly figure, clad in full plate armour and chain mail and flanked by two ladies. The lady to his left has her hands joined in prayer, while his right hand is outstretched to clasp that of the other. This is the tomb of John Hawley and his two wives: Joan and Alice. It is his first wife, Joan, whose hand he holds. John Hawley, the second of three fourteenth-century Dartmouth men to bear that name, died on December 30th 1408, probably at his house nearby, and was duly buried in pride of place in the church of which he was one of the early benefactors. The inscription on the brass refers to him as the *"founder of this chancel"*.

Chaucer and Hawley were men of exactly the same time and of broadly similar origins. Both were men of the world, served their kings through turbulent times and became prominent within their respective fields of endeavour. Chaucer's professional life spanned the latter part of the assertive reign of Edward III and the turbulent times of Richard II, while Hawley survived well into the reign of the troubled usurper, Henry IV. Chaucer achieved huge and enduring celebrity and has been the subject of numerous detailed biographies, while Hawley's image persists only in a brass engraving, a vague, local folk memory and in the writings of a small number of local and specialist historians.

The two men may, however, in one respect share a common immortality – as imagined pilgrims in the pages of *The Canterbury Tales*. Chaucer, of course, casts himself as the rather self-mocking narrator of the story, whilst Hawley, in spite of the very different image portrayed on his memorial brass, may well have provided the inspiration for, or been the satirical object of, Chaucer's characterisation of the Shipman who joined the pilgrims on their journey.

Chaucer's own life did not lack drama and he certainly encountered more than his share of larger-than-life characters, but it seems that his dealings with some of the maritime adventurers of his day left a lasting impression. Here, from the general prologue of his masterpiece, we see the fourteenth century mariner through his eyes:

A SHIPMAN was ther, wonynge fer by weste;	There was a SHIPMAN, living far out west;
For aught I woot, he was of Dertemouthe.	For all I know, he was of Dartmouth.
He rood upon a rouncy, as he kouthe	He rode a nag, as best he could,
In a gowne of faldyng to the knee.	In a gown, of thick woollen cloth to his knee.
A daggere hangynge on a laas hadde he	A dagger hanging on a cord had he
Aboute his nekke, under his arm adoun.	About his neck, under his arm, and down.
The hoote somer hadde maad his hewe al broun,	The hot summer had made his colour brown,
And certeinly he was a good felawe.	And certainly he was a good fellow.
Ful many a draughte of wyn had he ydrawe	Many a draught of wine had he taken
Fro Burdeux-ward, whil that the chapman sleep.	Of Bordeaux, while the merchant slept.
Of nyce conscience took he no keep.	Conscience did not concern him.
If that he faught, and hadde the hyer hond,	If he fought and had the upper hand,
By water he sente hem hoom to every lond.	He sent them home by water to every land.
But of his craft, to rekene wel his tydes,	But of his craft, to calculate the tides,
His stremes, and his daungers hym bisides,	The currents and the dangers around him,
His herberwe and his moone, his lodemenage,	His harbours, and his moon, his pilotage,
Ther nas noon swich from Hulle to Cartage.	There was none such from Hull to Cartagena.
Hardy he was, and wys to undertake;	Hardy and wise in his undertakings;
With many a tempest hadde his berd been shake.	By many a tempest had his beard been shaken.
He knew alle the havenes as they were,	He knew all the havens as they were,
From Gootlond to the Cape of Fynystere,	From Jutland to Cape Finisterre,
And every cryke in Britaigne and in Spayne.	And every creek in Brittany and Spain.
His barge ycleped was the Maudelayne.	His barge was called the *Maudelayne*.

The seemingly improbable connection between the Shipman thus described and the grand and expensively armoured figure of the engraving will be discussed later herein, but it should be stated at the outset that John Hawley was much more than just an ordinary merchant seaman who happened to cross the path of the great poet and inspire this description.

The West Country has a famous maritime and naval tradition and Hawley was perhaps the earliest prominent figure with whom it can be associated. The men of Devon were involved in fights at sea before Hawley sailed, often with one another, but it was not until around the time that he appeared that they had the wherewithal to mount organised privateering campaigns and that such activity was to become the principal *raison d'être* of whole towns. A strong case can be made for Dartmouth, as it emerged in the fourteenth century, having been Devon's first ever naval port and for Hawley, although it was never a title which he bore, having been the first real Westcountry admiral.

The voyages of Elizabethan seamen such as Drake and Raleigh and the Napoleonic War exploits of the likes of Edward Pellew are well known. They were members of organised navies, exploring and travelling the world, fighting battles with cannon, musket and sword in a manner that has been so many times described and portrayed that often clichéd images of them have found their way into popular culture. These were, of course, multi-faceted personalities but they are remembered as quintessentially romantic, fighting sailors, their status as heroes surviving into posterity. It is tempting to regard Hawley as a kind of early prototype for these Westcountry mariners and, in some ways, he was. Like them, he fought at sea and, as with them, his actions at sea were sometimes controversial. But he was also a merchant, a mayor and a Member of Parliament and he operated as a privateer in a way which can, for the most part, be regarded as unique to the time and the place in which he lived. It should also be said that many of the sea actions with which his name was associated took place in his absence and that he only came to resemble the fighting sea captain in the classic mould in his later years.

The kind of blue-water voyaging of which Drake was a pioneer and which had, by the time of Pellew and Nelson, become, if not routine, at least well within the capabilities of any experienced naval captain, were quite unimaginable to Hawley. Although he spent his life in more or less constant motion, his geographical sphere of action was much narrower than theirs. He travelled often but there is no specific record of his ever having ranged further than London or the western coastal regions of France and, for all the estates which he acquired in Cornwall and elsewhere in his later years, Dartmouth was unquestionably the centre of his world. The story of Dartmouth in the latter part of the fourteenth century is the story of John Hawley, and vice versa.

Dartmouth occupied a more important place in the life of the English nation during Hawley's lifetime than it ever has done since. Its shifting population confronted war and pestilence with a dogged resilience, led by a group of confident oligarchs of which John Hawley was the undisputed and charismatic leader. He lived his whole life in a time of war, albeit one punctuated by edgy and often unreliable truces. He shone brightly at that time and in that place because a combination of political, economic, geographical and technological factors created unique challenges and opportunities to which he responded with a brilliant energy.

This is the story of a terrible time, an exciting place and an extraordinary man.

Chapter One:

The Place

"...of Dertemouthe"

To the hill-dwelling Saxon farmers, it had been an unpromising place. The steep-sided river valley was punctuated only by muddy creeks, alternately filling and emptying with a sixteen-foot tide. There was almost no usable, flat land and, where the settlement would eventually take root, a steep slope descended five hundred feet to a place where two creeks faced each other across the tideway – three quarters of a mile of mud, in turn divided and filled by a body of water never less than a quarter of a mile wide.

A few fishermen made their living there but most regarded the river as nothing more than an obstruction to their mobility. It was, to them, a dangerous place and they named it Dœrentamuthan – 'the mouth of the dangerous river'. The earliest known reference to the place, in the Anglo-Saxon Chronicle, was also sinister in its tone. The story goes that Biorn, a nephew of King Cnut, was treacherously abducted and taken to Dartmouth, where he was murdered and 'deeply buried'. A forbidding place, then, and scarcely even a place of habitation until well after the Norman Conquest.

The arrival of the Norman aristocracy, whose domains straddled the sea, occasioned a very different view of this muddy-sided estuary. Its steep hills sheltered a deep, safe, natural harbour and its tidal creeks provided for the beaching, repair and, eventually, the building of the ships that conveyed them to and from their continental lands. William of Normandy divided up the spoils of his conquest among his followers, taking care to ensure that none was so wealthy or dominant in any locality so as to be able to challenge his authority, but the Saxon demesne boundaries in the locality remained largely unchanged. The estates which included and were to the south of what was to become the port of Dartmouth were granted to one Walter of Douai, from whose origins in Flanders the name of the nearby village of Stoke Fleming derived. The poor, hilltop estate of Townstal was sub-let to one 'Ralf' and the land which gave onto the slate cliffs and rocky coves by the river mouth to 'a woman'.[1] By 1166, Townstal had passed into the hands of the Fitz Stephan family, who were to control it from their small manor house at Norton for a hundred and fifty years.

The Fitz Stephan lands extended down to the river's edge and to a part of the steeply sloping ground known as Clifton, to the south. Clifton was separated from the promontory of Hardness to the north by a deep valley containing a wide tidal inlet and it was here, as the tide permitted, that the people started to build the dam that they called La Fosse. The Norman French émigrés had experience in the construction of tidal mills and it was probably under the Fitz Stephans that the dam was built across the neck of the inlet between Clifton and Hardness for that purpose. The tide flowed in through an inlet duct ('la golet') which was closed at high water and then flowed out through the mill sluices. The dam not only created a pool to power the mill but a causeway that gave more convenient access between Clifton and Hardness than did the ford at the upper end of the valley. It also formed a hard base from which wharves could be extended outwards into the deeper part of the stream, providing much improved berthing for small ships.

Although, or perhaps because, the wheaten loaf was still a comparative luxury at this time, flour milling was a lucrative business; sufficiently so as to warrant the capital expenditure necessary to build the dam. The mill was probably built by the Fitz Stephans and it was certainly in their ownership in 1296. On October 7th of that year we see the (probably impecunious) Gilbert Fitz Stephan granting:

> "...to Philip Rurde and Constancia his wife the mill of Hardenasse with all milling and service...together with the fosse of the said mill...and even the pool of the said mill...Rendering annually to the chief lords a rose*: with reversion to the heirs of Philip. For which Philip paid 200 pounds sterling"[2]

This was a substantial capital outlay on Rurde's part but the business was by then a going concern and evidently profitable enough to survive in the ownership of the same family for many years. It was one of Philip Rurde's heirs, William, who granted land adjacent to the mill in 1344 to John Hawley's parents for the extension of their quay by the fosse.

The waters of the Dart were, however, by this time being used for much more than fishing and the powering of a flour mill. Medieval shipyards were modest affairs and little archaeological evidence of their existence survives anywhere, but

---

* *Roses, sometimes specifically red or double roses, appear frequently as token payments in deeds of this time, as do pairs of white gloves, often to be rendered at Christmas or Easter annually.*

the fact that one hundred and sixty-four ships had assembled at Dartmouth in 1147, prior to their departure for the Second Crusade, strongly suggests that it was by then a working port, with facilities for ship repair and maintenance[*]. Further evidence is provided by the appearance in the local records of surnames denoting nautical trades. Among the more commonplace names such as Richard the Baker, Oliver the Taverner and Richard the Tailor, we see for example, Ralph le Korker (caulker) and, most tellingly, in 1233, Martin le Coggare – a builder of cogs. Lest there be any doubt about the trade of the Coggares, Coggers, Koggares or Cogkeres, a deed signed by one *"Henry le Cogger, son of Brunkelot and Beatrix de Sede"* in 1300 bears his seal, which shows a high-prowed ship with a single mast.[3]

The maritime links between Dartmouth and France might have weakened over time, as the Norman migrants became anglicised, had it not been for the marriage, in 1153, of Henry II to Eleanor of Aquitaine. Eleanor's lands accounted for a large part of what is today France, dwarfing the territory of France itself (the Île de France), to whose king the lords of Aquitaine nonetheless owed fealty. As a result of the marriage, the king of England became overlord of Guienne[†], with its great port of Bordeaux, but the duty of homage which accompanied this was to sow the seeds of more than a century of conflict. For the time being, however, the renewal of strong dynastic links across the sea firmly established the position of Dartmouth as a significant port, favourably situated, as it was, for trade with Bordeaux.

Nor did it matter that overland transport to and from the town remained difficult and was for many years to continue to depend on packhorses rather than wheeled vehicles. Once the shipmen gained a toehold on the steep shoreline and started reclaiming land from the mud to build their quays, most of the material required for the business of the port, whether iron from Spain, cordage from Bridport[‡] or sailcloth from Brittany could be brought in by sea. Dartmouth was not a major destination in itself, but became an entrepôt and a place of sailors, shipbuilders and repairers. It also, by way of the river, was accessible to the wool and cloth exporters of Totnes and the tinners of Ashburton.

The predisposition of local barons to levy fines and duties on anything that moved within their lands soon became a cause of dispute as these trades developed. William de Cantiloupe (or Cantelowe), who had acquired the barony of Totnes through marriage, was in the mid-thirteenth century claiming the right to levy duties on goods transported via the waters of the Dart, as far as the sea. This was challenged by local traders in 1275, when a jury found that he had no right to do so. The record of the proceedings in this trial gives a clue as to the nature of the goods

---

[*] *There was, until the mid-twentieth century, a tradition of shipbuilding and repairing to the north of Hardness and it is likely that medieval shipbuilding and repairing were located on the shore there.*

[†] *The territory of Guienne varied over the centuries but was synonymous with Gascony at this time.*

[‡] *Bridport was the major centre of ropemaking in England although Russell (op.cit. p.22) states that there was once a ropewalk to the north of the mill pool in Dartmouth. A "Rauf Ropere" also appears in the poll tax returns for 1377.*

traded at that time, listing grain, beans, iron stanchions, herring, conger, and 'Irish boards', in addition to the major commodities – wool and wine. [4]

The Dartmouth shipmen also, it seems, had to contend with some extremely aggressive competition from mariners elsewhere along the coast. In spite of its unhelpful topography and lack of a safe anchorage, the men of the small port of Lyme in Dorset were at this time also endeavouring to develop their business and their rivalry with the Dartmothians became more than a little heated in 1264, resulting in what was evidently a very vicious sea fight. Henry III appointed two commissions of enquiry into this serious breach of the peace, the order appointing the second of which, issued at Gloucester on May 4th 1265, is the more revealing:

> *"Commission to Martin de Littelbiry, John de Aure and Simon de Grindham to enquire by the oath of men of Dorset as well as of Devon touching a fight lately had on the sea between the men of Lim and the men of Dertemue wherein beatings, woundings, homicides and other trespasses on both sides were perpetrated, and the king has commanded the sheriffs of those counties to attach those whom they find guilty and give the names of and have the bodies of these before the king on the quinzaine of Holy Trinity wherever he may be in England, to answer for the said trespasses"*[5].

Although neither the causes nor the judicial outcome of this incident are known, the enmity between the men of Lyme and Dartmouth was to persist for many years.

By the time the first John Hawley appeared on the scene, this place, which the Saxons had regarded as almost worse than useless, had become, by medieval standards, a substantial town and an important and strategic port. Consequently, its ownership had become a matter of some interest and its inhabitants had begun to flex their commercial and political muscles.

The area at the southern extremity of that part of the emerging town which clung to the hillside to the south of the Fosse and was known as Clifton abutted land held by the lords of Stoke Fleming and so, in order to distinguish it from Clifton-Fleming, it was named Clifton-Dertemuth. The Fosse thus came to link the two parts of what, under the ownership of the Fitz Stephans, coalesced, by 1250, into the town known as Clifton Dartmouth Hardness. In a conveyance of that year, Gilbert Fitz Stephan refers not only to "*my mill*" but also to "*my burgesses of Dertemue*"[6], implying that it was already, in effect, a borough whose burgesses paid court to him at Norton. It was not, however, to remain the property of the Fitz Stephans for very much longer.

Gilbert was often strapped for cash and, in 1293, he mortgaged[*] Townstal, including Norton and Dartmouth, to Nicholas of Tewkesbury, a clerk to the king[7]. The relationship between the two men turned out badly for Gilbert as, not only

---

[*] *In the indenture, signed at Southwark, Gilbert "granted" the land to Nicholas. It must, however, have been a mortgage because Gilbert continued to be referred to as the lord of Norton etc.*

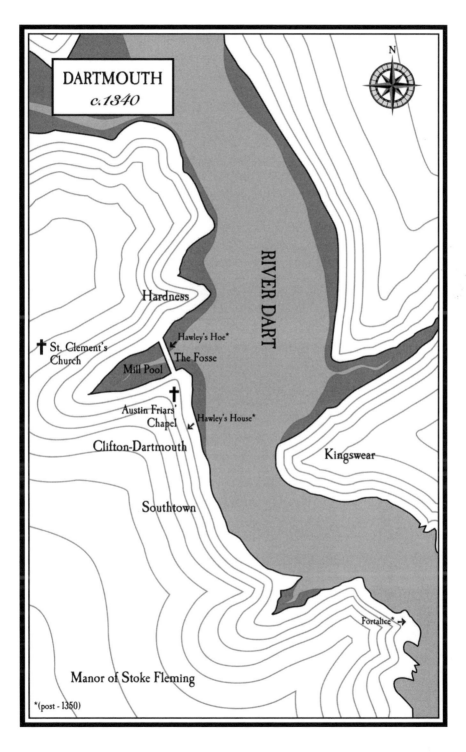

was his wife, Ysota, subsequently found to have had an adulterous relationship with Nicholas (to which Nicholas admitted), but he was also unable to redeem the mortgage, and the ownership of Dartmouth thus passed to Nicholas of Tewkesbury at some time before 1316.

Before the lordship of the town passed to Nicholas, however, Gilbert's burgesses had made significant progress towards being recognised as having significant authority in their own right. On May 25th 1270, Henry III ordered:

> *"Grant to the burgesses and merchants of Dertemue that they shall have for ever throughout the king's realm and power this liberty that neither they nor their goods be arrested for any debt whereof they are not sureties or principal debtors, unless the debtors are of their commune and power having wherewith to pay the debt in the whole or in part and the burgesses by whom the town is ruled fail to do justice."[8]*

The burgesses were thus acknowledged by the king as an organised body 'ruling' the town but it was not until 1327, when Nicholas gifted the borough to the young Edward III and was granted a pension for life in return, that Dartmouth became the royal borough that it was to remain.

Dartmouth became a civic entity which was in the king's gift as a result of this transaction and, in 1335, Edward granted lordship over it to Joan, the wife of John de Carew, the lord of Stoke Fleming, in recognition of her services to the king and to Queen Philippa. However, after the outbreak of the Hundred Years War, the king decided that he needed to have a close associate overseeing the affairs of what had, in effect, become an important naval port. He therefore decreed on February 9th 1341 that, on Joan's death, the town which, under the terms of the deed, was to have reverted to the Crown, should pass instead to Guy de Bryan – "*our beloved groom*". This was a mere diplomatic nicety as, on the same day, Joan obligingly granted the lands to Guy with immediate effect and appointed attorneys to deal with the paperwork, which was completed a year later.

Edward's strategic intentions were again to the fore when, two months later on April 14th, in the town's royal charter, he granted the liberties of …

> *"…the Mayor and Community of the Borough of Clyfton Dertemouth and Hardenasse…and even on account of the fact that the said our Burgesses undertake to furnish, grant and find two ships of war bearing one hundred and twenty tons and manned with double the equipment as much as other ships of our realm to assist in our following in the war…staying for forty consecutive days."[9]*

In return for the provision of this costly maritime service, the mayor and burgesses were thus granted extensive powers to rule the borough and were specifically exempted from no fewer than eighteen arcane types of fine and duty whose names read like the contents of the cupboards of a medieval apothecary.* The municipal seal which was appended to the document, which shows the king sitting in a ship with a raised poop and a smaller forecastle, over which stood a trident, is symbolically resonant with the nature of the deal. Dartmouth's first mayor, thus empowered and elected at Michaelmas 1341, was William Bacon, a man whose name had headed the list of burgesses since 1336.

The royal charter, however, reflected either a political oversight on the part of Edward, or careless drafting, because it omitted any mention of the fealty owed by the burgesses to Guy de Bryan, the loyal standard bearer and Knight of the Garter to whom the king had granted the borough just two months earlier. This oversight gave rise to the document in which the name Hawley – as a signatory – first appeared. De Bryan's complaint, and the way in which the dispute was resolved, were outlined with commendable brevity in an indenture of March 14th 1343, which was subsequently ratified at Westminster on May 18th of that year:

> "…and whereas the king, by charter dated 14 April, in his fifteenth year, granted to the burgesses and their successors divers liberties; subsequently because Guy asserted that these liberties for the most part would be prejudicial to him and his lordship and were contrary to the charter of the king to him therein, an agreement has been made between Guy and the mayor and burgesses, to wit… the mayor and burgesses grant that he and his heirs may have a steward at their will within the borough: Guy grants that the commonalty shall in every year elect a mayor and bailiffs to be sworn before him or his steward; the mayor and burgesses grant that the steward for the time being with the mayor shall hear and determine all pleas real or personal emergent there or affecting the liberty of the borough, and the steward and the mayor shall make all executions … and in case they cannot agree it shall be lawful for the steward to proceed as used to be done in the time of Nicholas de Teukesbury…"[10]

Although this indenture stipulated that the mayor and burgesses still owed fealty to De Bryan and that he still held some rather more than nominal authority over them, there is no record of him or any of his successors in title ever appointing a steward in Dartmouth and, by the time that John Hawley became mayor in 1374, there could have been no doubt in anyone's mind as to who was running the town.

---

* These included "theolonium" (a duty payable at markets and fairs), "pavagium" (writs ordering the repair of roads) "muragium" (a wall tax), "stallagium" (a fee for a plot or stall), "culagium" (requirement to ask the lord's permission to marry) and the seemingly onerous "lastagium" (a fee paid in order to be allowed to carry things where one would).

Burgesses and Merchants

'The burgesses and merchants of Dertemue', as Henry III's order of 1270 had called them, had long been one and the same; and they were burgesses because they were merchants and not the other way around. The royal charter, for all the potential constraints imposed by the indenture of 1343, had strengthened the grip which the merchant-burgesses had on the town and, as the young John Hawley was growing up, they were managing its affairs with increasing confidence. All towns in England, whether large or small, had emerged as effective oligarchies by the end of the fourteenth century, and it was during this period of consolidation of local mercantile power that Hawley grew to adulthood.

By combining mercantile activity and municipal duty, the burgesses of Dartmouth may rightly be thought to have skilfully positioned themselves in order to protect and further their own business interests in a competitive, litigious and sometimes dangerous environment. In doing so, however, they also took on responsibility for managing every aspect of the life of a town which, for much of the fourteenth century, combined the characteristics of a booming maritime-commercial marketplace, naval dockyard and front-line armed camp. In addition to the resident population, the town was host to waves of transient visitors, some of whom, as has been the case with seaports throughout history, were apt to be troublesome. The mayor and burgesses were responsible for upholding the criminal law, enforcing the regulation of traders, overseeing property transactions, organising the defences of the town and, increasingly often, arresting ships for the royal service and complying with other official orders and commissions. In addition to this, they had to deal with the aristocracy and the church. The roles of mayor and bailiff were by no means sinecures.

The mayor was elected annually at Michaelmas (September 29th) and held a court on the following Monday, at which a jury was sworn. At the second court of each mayoralty, a constable was appointed with responsibility for keeping the peace in Hardness, and two were charged with the same duty on the other side of the fosse in Clifton, which was effectively the town centre. The constables were only required to work on weekdays as, for some reason, criminal activity seems to have been deemed unlikely on the Sabbath. Also appointed were two assessors of the court, two ale-tasters and two church wardens.

Local trade regulations dictated that, for example, the miller was not allowed to keep pigs, geese or ducks, just *"3 hennys and a cok"*, in order that he might not be tempted to pilfer his customers' grain for use as feed. There were also strict delineations between trades. A shoemaker could not tan his own leather, while the fellmongers' trade itself was subject to regulatory demarcation, in that tanners could not cure the hides of sheep, horses, goats, dogs or deer; this work being reserved to the 'white tawer' or 'whittawer'.

The punishment of lawbreakers was generally left to the mayor and the bailiff, although a large court with a sworn jury was held every year on May 3rd. More serious cases were perhaps reserved for this assembly. Punishments for infringement of trading rules appear to have been different according to the trade in question. Fishmongers were put in the stocks, whilst most dishonest tradesmen would be pilloried. Brewers who did not give full measure were singled out for particular treatment; they were first ducked in the river using the *'cukkyngstole'* before being put in the pillory to dry off.[11]

The gruesome punishments meted out to traitors and other major criminals at this time are well known, and such was their severity that juries were generally reluctant to convict those accused of serious offences. Executions in Dartmouth were therefore probably quite rare, although it is known that hangings took place at a crossroads at the top of the hill, a junction which is still known as Deadman's Cross. The only instance of capital punishment in the town at this time which is known to us was recorded because a legal technicality caused it to be drawn to the attention of a higher authority. On June 14th 1390, the king granted:

> *"Pardon to Richard Henri, burgess of Dertemuth and this year mayor – before whom and the coroner, on view of the body of William Beaumont, a jury of the town found that Denys, his wife poisoned him (for which she was indicted and condemned) – for burning the said Denys without express commission of the King, as done through negligence and not through malice, he firmly believing the town's privileges and liberties allowed it without any such commission; and restitution to him of his forfeited goods, if any."[12]*

On what evidence, if any, other than a corpse which presumably showed clear signs of poisoning, Mistress Beaumont was convicted and burned at the stake is not recorded but this incident seem to indicate approximately where the limits to the powers of the municipality lay. What form of execution would have been officially sanctioned as normal or why the burgesses were deemed to have acted beyond their powers in this instance is unclear. It is unlikely that a commission of the king would have been required to perform any execution and it may just have been a requirement when the condemned person was a woman or possibly that there was something which related to the status of Beaumont herself which necessitated that her execution be sanctioned by a superior authority. Women were generally not hanged for serious crimes until well into the fifteenth century and most medieval codes of justice prescribed burning or drowning as ways of female execution. It is not known whether or not John Hawley, who was mayor in both the previous and following years, played any part in the handing down of this savage, but apparently conventional, sentence.

The records of the property transactions of the time have survived largely intact and give a detailed picture of the development of the settlement, of the ways in which the growing population managed the problems of living together in such a small space and how they started to expand that space by reclaiming land from the mudflats at the river's edge. These documents provide an incidental but useful and dynamic 'Who's Who?' of the burgesses because they were typically witnessed and signed in some order of precedence. When combined with the poll tax returns for 1377, they also give some indication of the transience of a significant number of the individuals who were the minor players in the story of John Hawley's life. It is noteworthy, for example, that some of the ships' masters and crewmen who are mentioned in connection with actions at sea in Hawley's and other Dartmouth ships during the latter part of the century appear neither in the poll tax returns nor anywhere else in the local record[*]. Some of the names that do appear suggest that they were comparatively recent migrants. The poll tax return, for example, lists two men named Breton, a Philip Irlond, a Thomas Irischman and a number whose names suggest that they had Cornish origins. The return excluded the 'obviously mendicant', among whom migrants might be expected to be comparatively numerous.

If, in addition to the steady stream of workers from the countryside, upon which all towns at the time depended, fourteenth-century Dartmouth played host to large numbers of visiting mariners, mercenary soldiers, traders and feckless agricultural vagrants, the municipality appears to have been well prepared to cope with any trouble which such inflows may have occasioned. And, although, as individuals, they may have had regular altercations with the authorities with regard to their maritime activities, the mayor and burgesses as a body also seem to have managed their relationships with the king and aristocracy smoothly and skilfully most of the time. It is perhaps ironic, then, that some of their most protracted and difficult negotiations were with the feudal first estate – the church.

The church in the fourteenth century was rich, powerful and political and it held considerable sway over the lives of people of all classes. Church attendance was compulsory and considerable efforts were made, and considerable sums spent, on anything which might smooth the path to eternal salvation. The various factions within the church vied for authority and the right to say mass or conduct other religious rituals was jealously guarded. The church of St Clement at Townstal had been the parish church since the times when the settlements in valley below had consisted of nothing but a few fishermen's huts by the shore at Hardness but, as the majority of the population by the mid-thirteenth century lived down near the river, this had become very inconvenient. The often slippery path from the Fosse at Hardness to the church door measured half a mile and rose some three hundred and fifty feet, and the parishioners, by reason of the 'very great fatigue of their bodies' asked to be allowed to build a church next to the water at Clifton.[13]

---

[*] *The poll tax was levied on all over 14 years of age. Exclusion of some of these seamen from the 1377 return may, therefore, just signify that they were very young at that time.*

They took the opportunity of a visit by Edward I to the town in 1286 to petition him in this regard and Roger Bacon, a local landowner and forebear of the town's first mayor, was authorised to assign an acre of land for the building of a new church in Clifton to the Convent of Torre, within whose jurisdiction the parish fell. The Canons of Torre, however, fearing that the existing church would fall into disuse, demurred and the parishioners continued to make the climb on every Sunday and holy day of obligation. A crisis arose and local passions were inflamed when the vicar of Townstal committed suicide by drowning in 1329 and the church was closed by order of the bishop for two years. All church services, christenings, weddings and funerals ceased during that period. When St Clement's re-opened in 1331 the bishop compromised regarding the Dartmothians' pleas, but only to the extent of allowing mass to be said for aged and infirm parishioners at the small chapel of St Clarus, which overlooked the mill pool in Hardness and was only a hundred or so yards up the hill.

The public-spirited William Bacon (a son of Roger), however, persisted in seeking a more satisfactory arrangement and obtained a licence to donate his acre of land to the Austin Friars in order that they might build an oratory and dwelling houses thereon. The friars duly commenced construction but the project incurred the wrath of the bishop, who ordered proceedings to be taken against the brothers and excommunicated Bacon. The friars appealed to the Vatican but eventually received a papal order to demolish their chapel in 1344. For some reason they took no action and, meanwhile, came an unexpected and bizarre intervention.

In March of that year, William Bacon and the then mayor, William Smale, were pleased to welcome one 'Brother Hugo' who had arrived in the town in layman's clothing and armed with a sword but had promptly gone to the friars' chapel and donned the habit of their order. He then placed a mitre on his head and announced to the gathered congregation that he was the Bishop of Damascus, a claim which, however improbable, would have been difficult to dispute. He proffered a ring which he claimed had been given to him by the pope and announced that the friars' appeal had been successful and that he had been sent by the pontiff to consecrate the chapel, which he duly affected to do, sprinkling holy water around the building. He then heard confessions, confirmed children and absolved some who had been excommunicated for crimes of violence, rounding off a good day's work with a celebratory drink with the mayor and William Bacon. One act of absolution which he had felt obliged to make during the day was of a sailor who, mistaking him for the Abbot of Torre, who was presumably unpopular in the town, struck him with a bow and threatened further violence.

It was all, however, too good to be true and Hugo was subsequently arrested at Exeter and exposed as a fraud. He had apparently studied at Cambridge and had become interested in cases such as that involving the friars' chapel but had no connection at all with either the Vatican or Damascus. Just who Hugo was and why he had taken it upon himself to intervene in this strange way on behalf of the parishioners is unknown, but the consecration was clearly a sham and, although some concessions were made to the friars in the interim, it was not until the appointment, in 1372, of the pragmatic Bishop Brantyngham – who was simultaneously dealing with the local shipowners and burgesses on matters temporal – that a deal was finally struck, allowing the consecration and expansion of the friars' chapel. Brantyngham dedicated the church to the Holy Trinity on October 13th of that year. John Hawley was a signatory to the document which recorded the consecration and was a major benefactor of the church in its early years.

Eighty-six years of clerical intransigence had cost the parishioners of Dartmouth dear in terms of shoe leather and aching limbs, but the burgesses had got their way in the end and the church in which John Hawley's remains were eventually to be interred was expanded and beautified by them during the years when he was the town's dominant figure.

The survival of extensive municipal records has afforded a reasonably clear view of the way in which the likes of John Hawley conducted their affairs as mayors, burgesses and borough officials, but there is much less material available which might shed light on their operations as the merchants which – first and foremost – they all were. This is not a problem which is particular to Dartmouth. Scholars of this period have struggled to discover how English merchants in general operated at a time when their operations were set about with unusual risks and when the legal and financial infrastructure supporting them was as yet very under-developed.

The merchants of Dartmouth were, for the most part, shipowners – a fact which probably placed them at or near the top of the mercantile hierarchy in terms of potential wealth. They were, however, remote from the main commercial action of the realm, insofar as London, with its numerous guilds and merchant companies, was inevitably dominant in many ways. As shipowners, they were providers of transport, but they also traded on their own accounts as principals, usually specialising to some degree in the commodities which naturally flowed along the routes plied by their ships. Even such semi-specialists, however, also engaged in a more miscellaneous trade and developed commercial links and supply channels in a wide range of businesses.

One may be inclined to think of the Dartmouth men, the nature of whose trade varied from year to year and took place across a comparatively wide geographical compass, as merchant adventurers, but that term more correctly applies to the organised companies which were formed in later years to promote a lucrative and highly speculative trade with more distant parts of the world. But neither were they involved purely with the staple trades, continuously and almost routinely shipping wool or tin to Calais, Flanders or wherever the designated monopsony of the Staple was located at the time. The pattern of their trade was further complicated by their strategic military location and the calls which the king made upon them from time to time for logistical support.

With all of this in mind, one is prompted to ask how all this complex and expensive activity was financed and how accounts were settled. There existed by the mid-fourteenth century a network of markets across the whole of England, with an established silver coinage providing for a cash economy, but the commercial world occupied by the larger merchants, particularly those whose trade had an international element, was far more complicated than could be supported by this alone. Merchants collaborated closely at the local level, their business and social ties often even being reinforced by marriage, but they were also dependent on credit arrangements with counterparties elsewhere and of whom they had far more limited knowledge.

One unusually complete set of ledgers for the period when John Hawley was Dartmouth's leading merchant has survived and, although they are the accounts of a London ironmonger, they provide an insight into how trade was conducted by all such men at the time[14]. Gilbert Maghfeld, like Hawley, mixed business with local and, to some extent, national politics in that he was variously an alderman and sheriff of the City of London and was, for sixteen months in 1383-4, appointed guardian of the seas from Berwick to Winchelsea – a role for which he seems to have been rather under-qualified.

His records show that he specialised in iron, which he sourced mainly from Bayonne. This accounted for two-thirds to three-quarters of his trade at any time, but he also dealt in a wide range of other goods, which included wine, beaver, saffron, woad, alum, liquorice, canvas, linen, herring, millstones, silk, wainscot boards, lead, wax, copper and even asses from Spain. A good deal of Maghfeld's sales were direct to the end-user, whether it was wine to wealthy Londoners, lead to plumbers or iron to blacksmiths, reflecting his location at the centre of the largest population centre in the country. Many of the goods in which he dealt, however, were traded in exchange for other goods, with comparatively small cash settlements being made to balance the transactions. He purchased the iron which was his principal stock in trade by shipping grain and cloth to Bayonne, the ships returning with the iron and subsidiary ladings of wine, beaver, saffron, liquorice and other products of that region.

He used subordinate merchants and local agents who had specialist knowledge of the goods being bought and sold. He employed, for example, a specialist who bought fine wines for him in the area around Bayonne and he often entrusted this man with significant sums of cash for the purpose. From this it can be seen that fourteenth century merchants operated variously as principals and agents and that the value of cash transactions was reduced by a substantial element of barter. Some commodities, such as iron and wine, always, it seems, had such a ready market that it was invariably worth buying them for resale and, as such, where large transactions between merchants were concerned, they became near substitutes for cash. This kind of barter trade was useful because, although a banking system for the provision of mercantile credit was beginning to emerge in Italy at this time, no such facilities were available to English merchants. Where credit was required – and it most often was – it was provided by the traders themselves.

In Maghfeld's case – and we have no reason to believe that it would have been any different for the Dartmouth merchants – anything up to three quarters of his merchandise was sold on terms of deferred payment. Whether or not this extension of credit carried with it an agreed rate of interest or whether prices were adjusted to reflect the expected time-lag between delivery and payment is not known, but the total sums entered in the debtors' column in his accounts were substantial. At his death, Maghfeld was owed nearly five hundred pounds and, although the letters of obligation received as IOUs rarely allowed for more than three or six months credit, some of the debts owing to him had been outstanding for considerably longer and some, inevitably, were irrecoverable*.

Some of the most difficult debts to recover were those owed by the aristocracy and, ironically, the Crown. Richard II not only borrowed from City merchants, he also imposed substantial levies on them to finance his military campaigns. When, in 1394, preparations were in train for the Irish expedition, Maghfeld and two others were specifically charged with equipping the *George of the Tower*† and two other ships, both of which bore the name *Trinity*. The total cost of this was £360.9s.10¼d. and Maghfeld had still not been reimbursed eighteen months later. It was largely as a result of official impositions of this kind that Maghfeld's finances were in a parlous state at the time of his death.

The business of the Dartmouth merchants as principal traders was certainly as complex as that of Maghfeld and, in addition, most of them were shipowners. This obviously involved large, initial capital outlays for the building or purchase of ships but the indications are that, in favourable trading conditions, a ship could pay for itself in a year or less. It is easy enough to imagine the town's shipbuilders extending credit to shipowners and vice versa and debts being partly settled with consignments of wine, iron, timber, sailcloth or fish. It would be easier to extend credit and collect debts locally than with barely known counterparties elsewhere and the local merchant community would thus have been bound together financially as well as socially.

The Dartmouth in which John Hawley was born and raised was energetic, exciting and dangerous. The town's merchant class, of which his parents were members, was shaking off the shackles of the old feudal hierarchy and taking firm control of its own affairs. It was a close-knit, competent and resolute group but its competence and resolve were to be severely tested from the very early years of Hawley's life.

The last two documents in which John Hawley's name appeared during his lifetime were concerned with debts owed to him.

† A king's ship, as indicated by the suffix "…of the Tower".

Chapter Two:

The Times

A Dangerous Childhood

When Edward III sailed for home on urgent business on February 21st 1340 he did so without his queen, who was unavoidably detained in Ghent. There were pressing diplomatic reasons for Philippa's continued presence in Flanders but she was heavily pregnant and would probably have been ill-advised to accompany her husband on the journey anyway. Two weeks later, she gave birth to the couple's third surviving son, who was to bear the title of duke of Lancaster but was always better known by the name which he took from his birthplace. John of Gaunt was born on March 6th of that year.

The infant prince was unusual among the men of his time in that the date of his birth was noted for posterity, a distinction that was not accorded even to all of royal blood. For historians whose late medieval subjects, although perhaps no lesser men than John of Gaunt, were of lesser rank, educated guesswork of birth dates is the near-universal rule. We know that Gaunt, Geoffrey Chaucer and John Hawley were very close contemporaries. We know that most of their lives ran in parallel and, occasionally and in some ways, intersected but, for Hawley and even for Chaucer, we know neither the dates nor even the years when they were born. All that can be said is that more or less confident inferences can be drawn from analysis of the events of their later lives – their marriages, public appointments and feats of arms – and that, in the case of Hawley, this evidence has pointed to a birth date of approximately 1340. There is, at any rate, nothing in the story to be told hereafter which jars with that assumption and, while it would be satisfying to be able to say, for example, that John Hawley was welcomed into the world on a sunny Tuesday morning in May 1340, we cannot. We must shrug and get on with our story as best we can.

Our John Hawley was the second of that name. His father was a man of some substance but, were it not for the famous son, he would certainly have escaped the notice of historians altogether. His sole and minor claim to fame in his own right is that he was present at the birth of Dartmouth as a borough and he makes his first appearance as the ninth among the twelve burgesses who were signatories to the indenture with Guy de Bryan of March 1343, which laid out the terms of the co-existence between the borough and the feudal lord.

This was a time at which some of the free peasantry were being encouraged by the local lords to move into the villages and small towns of Devon and elsewhere, there to build up the infrastructure necessary to support the growth of industry and other aspects of local and national life. It is possible that the first John Hawley was a part of that movement. One historian suggests that he was a younger son of a free tenant farmer of the manor of Allaleigh, four miles to the north-west of Dartmouth in the parish of Cornworthy, and that, having no prospect of inheriting the family farm, he moved into the town, with his wife Elizabeth, some time before 1340, there to become a merchant and shipowner.[15]

Although there is little or no direct evidence to support this theory, it is very plausible. Surnames at this time were often toponymic, that is to say that men were referred to by their place of origin or residence, and the early references to 'Johan de Hawlee' are strongly suggestive of a connection with Allaleigh. A contemporary reference to one 'Richard de Capyton' similarly, if rather more transparently, denotes the nearby manor of Capton and a rendering of Allaleigh as 'Awlee' is also consistent with the way in which Devonians have corrupted their vowels and consonants in living memory.

How the Hawleys came by the capital necessary to set up their business is unknown. Most migration from the agrarian sector at this time was forced by overpopulation and actual or incipient destitution but, if his origins were indeed of this nature, John seems to have managed to make the transition to town life unusually comfortably, perhaps because the family farm was sufficiently large and productive to support a cash legacy to a younger son in lieu of a land inheritance. The use of 'de' in John's surname may also be indicative of membership of the minor gentry, whose younger sons also often found their way into trade at this time, and with some capital behind them. He was anyway of sufficient means by 1343 to rub shoulders with the other worthy signatories to the indenture and, on June 18th 1344, we are afforded our only clear glimpse of the apparently prosperous man behind that signature, in the following conveyance:

"William Rurde granted to John de Hawlee and Elizabeth his wife a place of land 20 feet wide in Clifton Dertemouth next to the mill which stands upon 'la fosse' between the quay of the aforesaid John and Elizabeth on the south and the intake stream (la-golet) of the aforesaid new mill on the north and from three feet of standard measure behind the said new mill on the west side of the aforesaid place and as much as they can protect against the sea on the east side. Rendering 4d. annually."[16]

From this we may infer that the John and Elizabeth already had an established business which required a quay, and a quay that they were expanding by leasing additional land and by reclamation. These were the origins of the famous 'Hawley's Haw' or 'Hawley's Hoe', which was to pass into local folklore in the form of the jingle:

"Blow the wind high, blow the wind low,
It always blows fair to Hawley's Hoe"

The picture is unmistakably one of an up-and-coming merchant family whose head was a respectable local burgess and possibly a shipowner. John appears again in the role of witness signatory to two land conveyances: one on June 28th and the other on July 5th, 1344. Then, as suddenly as they appeared, he and Elizabeth completely and permanently vanish from the record.

This is rather puzzling and, for the would-be Hawley biographer, inconvenient. There are a few possible explanations for the abrupt disappearance of a prosperous and well-connected, youngish couple but the lack of any direct evidence means that none of them can be embraced with total conviction.

It is possible that John survived in good health and for some reason withdrew from the more visible aspects of the life of the borough. The list of burgesses appearing in the local records for this early period is certainly less consistent in its composition than it was in the 1370s and later. Why this should be the case is not entirely clear. It was possibly just because the merchant population of the new and growing town was more mobile than it subsequently became but, equally, it is not difficult to imagine that, as the more competitively minded residents vied for advantage in a severely limited space, factional in-fighting may have broken out among the burgesses, increasing the rate of turnover within the group. Hawley's disappearance from the list of signatories to the business documents of the town may have resulted from some kind of falling-out with the other burgesses and a consequent decision to withdraw from civic life and to concentrate on his own business.

There is, however, a more persuasive and obvious explanation. Of the twelve signatories to the indenture of 1343, eight continued to show up elsewhere in the record until at least 1351 and one featured until 1378. The remaining four, including John Hawley, disappeared before 1351. Of the four, Hawley was the first to drop out of sight, while the others continued to put in occasional appearances until 1348. All four, the first John Hawley included, may have disappeared for any reason but there is one probable cause which looms large.

The catastrophe which struck Dartmouth in the early months of 1349, when the second John Hawley was perhaps eight or nine years old, was incomparably more traumatic and terrifying than anything which had happened there before or has happened there since. Every aspect of the calamity that was the Black Death was horrifying and its effects were to change the life of England for generations to come.

The pandemic probably had its origins in the bacillus *Pasteurella Pestis* which resided in the bloodstream of Manchurian marmots and other rodents in isolated parts of Central Asia. For some reason, these rodents and their attendant fleas migrated from their remote fastness around 1338 and set in course an inexorable spread of the disease into China and thence across the whole known world, arriving in Western Europe in 1347.

The most oft-cited account of the arrival of the plague in England, *The Grey Friars' Chronicle,* suggests that it arrived with the rats on one of two ships which docked at the port of Melcombe, now part of Weymouth, 'a little before the feast of St. John the Baptist' (June 24th) in 1348. The *Chronicle* suggests that the disease was brought from Gascony and that the men of Melcombe were the first in England to be infected with it. This may well be true but Dartmouth was at least as important a port as Melcombe at the time and, had the plague not spread overland in the few months that followed, it would only have been a matter of time before Dartmouth received its own directly imported pestilence. In any event, the disease marched steadily westwards and by the middle of 1349 virtually every village and town in Devon and Cornwall was affected.

The symptoms of the disease were horrible and, except in a tiny minority of cases, it was fatal. Everything about it was disgusting and degrading and it seemed to be designed to cause the maximum possible distress and social dislocation. It was easy to regard the victims with revulsion rather than pity and this, coupled with the knowledge that being in close proximity to a victim was quite likely to result in infection, had catastrophic effects within families and social groups. Tales of isolation and heroic self-quarantine at this time are legion and it is noteworthy that the group which suffered the highest death toll of all was the clergy, who were obliged by their calling to overcome their natural fears and to tend to the sick. One Devon deanery – that of Kenn near Exeter – suffered the highest rate of attrition among its clergy of any in the whole country, losing eighty-six incumbents from only seventeen parish churches.[17]

Direct records of mortality in the towns and villages of England are extremely sparse and Dartmouth is unexceptional in this respect. The surviving local records, which normally present quite a detailed picture of the life of the town, albeit through a somewhat narrow-angle lens, give no indication at all that the tragedy

The catastrophe of 1349 – the Black Death probably killed a third of the population of Dartmouth.
Illustration of bubonic plague from the Toggenburg Bible 1411

even occurred. All that can be said is that there are rather fewer entries of any kind for 1349 than for most years. What few entries there are portray an ordinariness which, given what we know of the circumstances, is touching. On March 20th 1349, at a time at which the pestilence was almost certainly at its height, and with friends and neighbours dying horrible deaths all around them, Ralph Bruwer, then mayor, and, among others, William Smale, gathered to witness a conveyance in which one Alicia Kene transferred her right in a Dartmouth tenement to John Wetene[18]. Life, it seems, went on.

It might be said that late medieval village and small town communities were, by their very cohesiveness, well suited to coping with a disaster such as this, insofar as any community ever could cope with it. The inhabitants of towns and villages across England strove to get on with business as usual and, although business was very far from usual, the pandemic did not result in the total socio-economic collapse which might be expected in other times or in less robust social systems.

Estimates of overall mortality rates in England during the Black Death vary, but a figure of around one third of the population is generally accepted. Bubonic plague generally resulted in a much higher death toll once a particular critical mass of population density was reached, and town dwellers accordingly suffered worse losses than did rural communities. Dartmouth, with its greater than average exposure to imported infection and its population crammed together on the river's edge, is likely to have been hit hard by the disease and the crude statistics are such that by far the most likely explanation for the disappearance of Hawley's father is that he was a victim of it.

We may add the caveat that the first appearance in the record of the second John in 1372 was also surprisingly abrupt and it may be that the public record is not as trustworthy an indication of the presence or absence of a prominent local figure as we may think. If so, it may be rash to infer his father's early death simply from his disappearance from the record. It is clear, however, that the first of the three John Hawleys did not survive long enough to be referred to as 'the elder'. That title was used exclusively in reference to the second John and it seems certain that something did happen to the father between the point at which he vanished in 1344 and his son burst on the scene in 1372 – most likely in the early part of that period and most likely during the plague of 1349. Further evidence that both John and Elizabeth were dead by August 1373 can be found in the local record for that date, when *"John Haulegh son of John Haulegh and Elizabeth his wife"* claimed the seisin* of a messuage† that had been conveyed *"...to the parents of John Haulegh"*[19].

The subsidiary role of women at the time means that the disappearance of Elizabeth from the record in the interim is less surprising and, if John did fall victim to the plague in 1349, there is no specific reason to believe that she also perished. Indeed, if she had died, it would have been difficult for her young and only son to have maintained the family name, carried on the business and appeared in the prosperous form which he displayed in later years. There is no sign that she remarried, as was quite common at the time, but she may just have been sufficiently strong, resourceful and well-supported to carry on overseeing the business while bringing up her only son.

Almost nothing is known about the wider Hawley family and it is therefore difficult to assess the likelihood that local family support would have been available to Elizabeth – or to John alone if his mother had also perished during the pestilence of 1349. A 'Thomas Hawle' appears, with his wife and one servant, in the poll tax return of 1377, in which John's name is also spelled as 'Hawle'. The two names reappear, together as witnesses to a document in January 1392[20], on this occasion both spelled as 'Hawlegh'. Although nothing more is known of him, this at least implies that Thomas Hawley was both reasonably affluent and well known to John and, although it has never been suggested that they were related, they may well have been. If so, it may be that Thomas's family helped to support John in his childhood or, if Elizabeth was dead, even that they adopted him until he was old enough to manage his own affairs.

---

* *Right of possession of land as a free man.*

† *dwelling*

There is strong evidence that one Richard Scoce, who was born around 1363, was a young cousin of John Hawley. A John Scoce, who it seems reasonable to speculate was Richard's father or, more likely, uncle, was a co-signatory with Hawley's father on the 1343 indenture, and was Dartmouth's bailiff in 1344, after which he also disappears from the record. If Richard was John's cousin, John Scoce may have been Elizabeth's brother, or a brother-in-law to the first John Hawley by marriage to some unknown sister. Neither John nor Richard Scoce appears in the 1377 poll tax return but a Joan Scot*, with one servant, does and it is possible that she was John Scoce's widow. Richard was resident in Southtown in 1391 and puts in a number of appearances as a junior burgess until 1399.

Both of these fragments suggest that Hawley may have had fairly affluent local relatives, on one or both sides of his family. This should not be surprising, given the way in which merchant families tended to inter-marry and, if true, could have provided a strong basis for John's upbringing if he had indeed lost one or both of his parents. The simultaneous disappearance of John Scoce and his putative brother-in-law, John Hawley, may signify that they both died in the 1349 plague and that the Hawley and Scoce families came together in mutual support afterwards. However, from what we know of the formidable personality of our John Hawley as an adult, it can certainly be imagined that, if he was living with a widowed mother or in the family of an uncle or aunt, he may have started to become actively involved in the family business at an early age and have been very much a self-made man by the time he appears in the record.

The community in which Hawley was brought up was possessed not only of the cohesiveness which was typical of the time but also of a sense of purpose which was driven by a dynamic which was far more forceful in Dartmouth than it was in the rural communities that surrounded it. Merchant families everywhere and throughout history have at once competed and cooperated with one another and, in the maritime-commercial hothouse which was Dartmouth in the middle part of the fourteenth century, a high degree of collaboration would have been necessary. The merchant and shipowner families of the town lived cheek by jowl and their business activities were constantly intertwined. The catastrophe which struck them all in 1349 would have left nobody untouched and the need for mutual support would have been felt more keenly than ever.

The adult Hawley was an exceptionally able and intelligent man and it is easy to imagine him as a precocious and positive child, but his formal education, like that of all around him, would have been very limited. The town was too small and distant from any of the larger centres of learning readily to support a school and

---

* *This name appears in various forms, including 'Scot' and 'Scoz', which suggest that it may have been pronounced as something like "Scotch", with implied Scottish origins. The Hawley-Scoce connection is clearly established in evidence given during the Roches v. Hawley trial described in chapter four.*

certainly there is no record of one existing there at the time. He may have received religious instruction from some local member of the clergy, but would probably have learned to read at home, from an ABC and then a primer that consisted of little more than a few basic prayers. Everything else he would have learned from the people around him.

Although the people around him, in such a small town, were of all segments of society, his immediate social circle would have consisted of seamen and merchants and it was from these people that Hawley would, quite literally, have learned his trade. Hawley was a lifelong member of a very close-knit community and some of the merchant families in the town lived and worked closely together over the course of two or more generations. The most obvious example of this was the relationship between the Hawleys and the Asshendens, which likely spanned three generations and could, had John not been raised by relatives, have provided the kind of substitute for extended family support which a young, fatherless boy would have needed. William Asshenden puts in his first appearance in the record a few weeks before that of Hawley's father, in January 1343, as the master of *la Seinte Marie Cog,* and became mayor of the town in 1359. If the first John Hawley, as putative shipowner, failed ever to appear in the admiralty courts and did not rise through the ranks of the burgesses to become mayor for the simple reason that he died while he was still a young man, there is much that can be seen in his son as an adult which might reflect Asshenden as a substitute paternal role model. The adult Hawley emerges as an energetically outgoing and collegiate operator, which in all probability reflected a genuine gregariousness, and it may be that this was a style which he developed in his youth, as he sought substitutes for what he had lost.

This process of inference and guesswork to fill the gaping void in the record between 1344 and 1372, however, can only be taken so far. Exactly what happened to the first John; what eventually became of Elizabeth; how and when the second John met Joan, his first wife; at what age and under whose guidance he took over the family business and how he emerged as such a prominent and successful figure in 1372 we do not know and probably never will.

It is unlikely that Dartmouth was visited by the plague only once. The outbreak which scoured England in 1348-9 was by far the worst but, once it had arrived, the pestilence kept on recurring. There were, in total, six further outbreaks in England during John Hawley's lifetime; each surely inflicting a painful reminder of that particular trauma of his childhood, but it was a threat with which he and his contemporaries had to learn to live.

The speed with which Dartmouth and places like it recovered from the plague reflected not only a resilient social structure but also the fact that, by killing so many, the pandemic had removed much of the population pressure on the productive economy. There has been much scholarly debate on the exact impact of the plague on rents, prices and wage rates in the latter half of the fourteenth century[21]and there can be no doubt that its economic effects were complex and far-reaching but there seems to be little doubt that, by removing excess or under-employed labour from the system, it had a purgative effect and, by increasing labour productivity, a generally beneficial effect on the prosperity of the survivors. Prices and wages both generally rose throughout the second half of the century and there was some consolidation of land holdings in the countryside and the process of agricultural enclosure accelerated somewhat. These were generally reflections of a strengthening, and not a weakening, economy.

Edward III – a forceful personality and superb soldier.
Illustration from Cassell's History of England 1902

The Black Death was a dreadful experience for Hawley and all the people of Dartmouth but it did nothing to diminish the community's vigour and it was the other great tragedy of the age – the war with France – that shaped his and their work and experience for the rest of the century and beyond.

The sea which John Hawley sailed now forms a clear, wide and undisputed border between England and France but, to Hawley and his compatriots, it represented something quite different. From the Narrow Sea, which had been the conduit for the Norman Conquest nearly three centuries earlier, to the stormy Western Approaches, the waters linked two kingdoms which were yet to be completely separated and whose separation was to be a long and bloody process. The French influence in England was still to be seen everywhere. Many of the lords of English manors, including that which encompassed Dartmouth, had French names; English kings and princes still spoke French at least as a second language and the king of England literally lorded it over substantial parts of France during much of John Hawley's lifetime. Trading links with Gascony were strong and substantial and the trade in Gascon wine was for many years the mainstay of ports like Dartmouth. It was, however, a relationship which became increasingly troubled as England, in effect, became more English and territorial issues eventually and inexorably led to war.

The territorial issues that were to be contested at such huge cost in human suffering defy simple description and were set about with arcane dynastic, legal, diplomatic, military and economic considerations, with occasional papal interventions to compound the complexity. The underlying issues of dynastic rivalry and raw power politics were such that conflict was perhaps inevitable and, over the course of a century and more, proved to be endemic. The principal underlying cause of mutual resentment between the Plantagenet kings of England and the Capetian monarchs in France concerned the possessions of the English crown in Gascony, which had been an actual or potential bone of contention for many years, but the situation was rendered more acutely dangerous by a combination of a dynastic accident in France and the troubled accession of a singularly vigorous and ambitious king of England.

The premature death of Charles IV of France in February 1328 created a situation in which, for only the second time in three hundred years, there was no heir apparent to the French throne. If women were barred from the succession – and this was to become the subject of a protracted and heated politico-legal debate – then the strongest claimant in the male line was Philip of Valois, a nephew of Philip IV and cousin to the late king. The lack of clarity regarding the question of succession through the female line, however, gave cause for a claim to be made on behalf of the first-born son of Philip's daughter, Isabella. Isabella, as a result of a marriage which had been designed to lessen the enmity between the two realms, had been, since 1308, queen consort of Edward II, and her son – and thereby potential claimant to the throne of France – was the future Edward III of England. The circumstances surrounding the young Edward's accession to the English throne in the previous year, however, had been such that no such claim was lodged on his behalf in 1328 and, in May of that year, Philip of Valois was crowned King Philip VI of France at Rheims.

Isabella despised her husband and, when she had travelled to France in 1325, ostensibly on a diplomatic mission on Edward's behalf, she had been joined there by her lover, Roger Mortimer. She refused to return, denouncing Edward, whom she accused of deserting her for his favourite, and possibly lover, Piers Gaveston. The young Prince Edward came under the control of Isabella and Mortimer when he too travelled to Paris, as the newly named duke of Aquitaine, to do homage to King Charles of France. Despite increasingly vocal demands from King Edward that Isabella should return to England and bring his son with her – and direct appeals and orders to the prince himself – she, Mortimer and the young Edward remained in France. There, to her husband's impotent fury, Isabella arranged the betrothal of Edward to Philippa, daughter of Count William of Hainault. Isabella's actions were, however, part of a much more ambitious plan – to seize control of the throne of England. She and Mortimer returned to England in 1326 with a small army of Hainaulter mercenaries, there to be joined by swelling numbers of Edward's many enemies, and led what soon amounted to a popular uprising against her estranged husband, who was eventually forced to abdicate in favour of his son.

Edward III was crowned in Westminster Abbey on February 1st 1327 at the age of fourteen. Mortimer was the king-maker but his intention was that it would be he, and not Edward, who would exercise royal power. The young king commenced his reign under a regency in which, although he played no formal part, Mortimer was the dominant figure. Mortimer and Isabella took control and set about enriching themselves and consolidating their position. Edward was still seven years short of the age at which he could by inalienable right rule without a regent and Mortimer and Isabella might have maintained their control of the situation. However, Edward, whose unease at the behaviour of his mother and her lover, particularly the manner in which they had usurped the royal power of his father, had turned to alarm, was possessed of a steely determination of his own and determined to retake control and rule in his own right. Edward found a like-minded and totally loyal supporter in Philippa, who encouraged his natural tendency to militaristic self assertion. She was a staunch ally and confidante when he most needed one and, while Isabella and Mortimer continued to hold sway, she comforted him in his frustration and growing sense of humiliation.

Philip VI of France, the legitimacy of whose claim to the throne was open to question.

Detail from a 14th century French manuscript

The two years that followed, during which the apparently unassailable *de facto* reign of Mortimer and Isabella was marked by factional intrigue and near civil war, were traumatic for Edward and for England. The story of how Edward eventually overcame and disposed of Mortimer is too Byzantine in its complexity to be retold here[*] but, when Mortimer was hanged for treason at Tyburn in November 1330, and Isabella was allowed to retire to Castle Rising in Norfolk, the young king, although still three years short of his majority, began to rule in his own right.

Isabella had been unable to assert claim to the throne of France on her son's behalf in 1328, but the potential for Edward to do so for himself remained, as did the ambiguity surrounding the legitimacy of the kingship of Philip VI, particularly in English minds. It was also, crucially, a factor in Philip's thinking. For Edward, the real value of his potential claim to the throne of France was that it weakened Philip's claim to Gascony and it is generally believed by modern historians that he would not have asserted it in the way in which he subsequently did had he not been provoked by Philip in a number of ways and, in particular, with regard to Gascony.

For the first few years of his reign, however, the young king of England was in no position to make any such assertion, whatever his thoughts and ambitions may have been. One of his first foreign policy initiatives, once freed of the yoke of Mortimer and Isabella, was to seek to calm French fears with regard to his position on Gascony. In March 1331, in response to a complaint from Philip that the form of homage

---

[*] *It is, nonetheless, a story well worth the telling; Ian Mortimer gives an excellent account in his The Greatest Traitor: The Life of Sir Roger Mortimer, 1st Earl of March – Ruler of England 1327-1330. Jonathan Cape 2003*

that he had paid with regard to his French possessions was inadequate, he made a statement which was intended to confirm his willingness to pay homage, as duke of Guienne, to the king of France, which carried with it a specific duty of military service. The inherent contradiction in this statement, in which a sovereign king of one realm promised fealty to another, albeit as a duke and not as a king, reflected the underlying ambiguity of the circumstances surrounding Gascony and this was not an issue which was to be resolved so easily.

Protracted negotiations on the status of the various regions of Gascony followed and, at first, the signs that a deal could be struck appeared promising. The sticking point, however, was to be the status of the Agenais, the region to the east of Bordeaux, between the Dordogne and the Garonne, which had been seized by Philip's father towards the end of the reign of Edward II. Philip, in the meantime, attempted to bolster his own political position within France by adopting an increasingly intransigent line and openly provoking Edward, who was his junior by nearly twenty years, whenever possible. The provocations included support for the Scots, with whom Edward was almost constantly at war, and acts of aggression against English shipping.

It all came to a head in 1337. While increasingly tetchy diplomatic exchanges continued, Edward started to make military preparations for what now seemed inevitable, and both his and Philip's envoys made the rounds of neighbouring European states in efforts to form or shore up alliances. In this process, Edward's principal assets were economic and, by renegotiating the terms under which English wool was exported to the looms of the Low Countries, and by the application of hard cash elsewhere, he built a substantial coalition against Philip, who appeared to be comparatively indecisive and unwilling to extend himself financially.

On May 3rd 1337, Edward led his troops on a rapid march northwards in an attempt to inflict a defeat upon the Scots which he hoped would be sufficient to remove the threat from that quarter, at least for the time being. He was in Stirling when the king of France finally made the move that was to initiate the long war. On May 24th Philip declared the duchy of Aquitaine confiscate. The king of England and duke of Aquitaine was thus given the choice of fighting or of conceding a substantial and valuable part of his lands. He was not the kind of man who would for long have contemplated the latter alternative. When, in July 1337, Philip followed through on his declaration by sending troops to attack castles in Gascony, the war effectively began.

Wool, Wine and Warfare

Edward took full advantage of the bargaining power that his control over the supply of English wool gave him in Brabant and Flanders, and the alliances thus forged provided him with both troops and a strategic base for his campaigns. In order to be close to the action, he moved with his queen and children to Antwerp soon after the war broke out. He therefore called more or less constantly upon logistical support from

English shipowners and, although he was acquiring provisions locally, he needed to ensure the security of his supply routes across the Narrow Sea. It was here that the sea war was focused in the early years and, with his resounding victory over the combined fleets of France and her allies at Sluys, Edward achieved ascendancy, if not dominance, in those waters. Sluys was unusual in that it was a premeditated, pitched battle between two fleets, but the more usual pattern of maritime warfare during the Hundred Years War was of small-scale mutual predation of a more or less organised kind but with no particular focus. Once declared, the war at sea was fought virtually wherever and whenever ships from the belligerents met, whether by accident or design.

The outbreak of war changed everything for the men of Dartmouth. The land war was often punctuated by truces or periods during which hostilities were suspended because the opposing sides lacked the wherewithal to join battle. By contrast, those at sea where often ignorant of, or simply ignored, such cessations, with the effect that the situation there had become, immediately and permanently, much more difficult and dangerous. Commercial shipping was from now on subject to more or less constant threat and the resources of the shipowners were often called upon to transport troops and their equipment, even, and perhaps especially, during lulls in the fighting. The business of Dartmouth's maritime traders had always been a hazardous one. The hazards were now elevated to an altogether higher level.

The eloquence of Chaucer in getting to the nub of the matter is such that he is often invoked in commentary on many facets of the human condition. That doyenne of medieval economic history, Eleanora Carus-Wilson, could not resist, when discussing the emergence of the concept of the merchant adventurer, quoting from *The Canon's Yeoman's Tale*, in which the canon says:

> "*Us moste putte oure good in aventure.*
> *A marchaunt, truly, may not ay endure,*
> *Truste me wel, in his prosperitee,*
> *Som tyme his good is drowned in the see,*
> *And som tyme cometh it sauf unto the londe.*"

Routine maritime trade, then, was a risky undertaking in itself, but the war with France meant that routine was to be the exception throughout the lives of the second and third John Hawleys. When truces extended over a number of years, as they did in the 1360s and 1390s, some semblance of normal trade resumed, but trading patterns had by then been permanently distorted by the hostilities. However, whether it was being conducted in the midst of a hot war or a tentative peace, the sea-borne trade of England in the fourteenth century was dominated by two commodities: wool and wine.

Edward III was able to buy his bridgehead at the Brabant port of Antwerp in 1337 and eventually to form an alliance with Flanders because the industrial towns of the Low Countries were heavily dependent on supplies of raw wool from England. The nature of the trade was, however, to change markedly during the course of the century, and the pace of change was particularly rapid during Hawley's lifetime. At the beginning of the fourteenth century, the bulk of wool exports were in the form of bales of raw wool, and those trading in it were typically Italian or Flemish. By the century's end, most English wool was turned into cloth made and exported by Englishmen.

The geopolitics of the wool trade and the wiry nature of the wool that grew on the backs of Devon sheep meant that Dartmouth was never a major wool or cloth exporting port. Such local production as there was of raw wool, and later cloth, centred on Totnes, which sits at the navigable head of the Dart, and it is likely that this trade had its origins at the nearby Cistercian abbey at Buckfast. The Cistercians were always the most commercially-minded of the monastic orders and it has often been said of them that they 'came to do good and did well'. They were experts in sheep husbandry and had for decades been selling their output to foreign wool merchants who toured England in order to purchase the clip of the monastic houses. The Buckfast flocks were probably sizeable, as the abbey was well placed near the lower slopes of Dartmoor, where sheep could, and still do, graze freely. The quality of the moorland sheep's wool, however, was comparatively poor and this, combined with the wool trade's near-umbilical connection with the Low Countries, meant that Dartmouth was relatively disadvantaged by its westerly location. When Edward III captured Calais, after an eleven-month siege in 1347, he expelled the local population and created an English colony which was to remain for two hundred years. The wool staple was moved to Calais but, although this was, with a fair wind, a day's sailing less distant than Antwerp, it was still twice as far from Dartmouth as it was from even Southampton.

The historical record of trading activity in and out of Dartmouth in this period is very limited and the practice of combining its ladings with those of the other surrounding ports in the customs records for Exeter obscures the picture somewhat. Nonetheless, it is clear that the western ports were minor players in the huge export trade in wool. London was by far the largest wool exporter, followed by Boston. Even Newcastle, in the years for which records are available, shipped ten to twenty times the amounts of raw wool and cloth which flowed out of Exeter. [22]

We can only guess by more general inference, and some very limited documentary evidence, what the 'normal' trade of the town and of the Hawleys was. The customs records shed light only on those parts of cargoes which were subject to duty, and much of the inevitable miscellany of items shipped is thus lost from view. It is certainly reasonable to assume that, for all that it lacked any substantial hinterland from which wool and woollen cloth could be sourced, a significant part of Dartmouth's export trade would have been in those commodities. Customs records for the port in 1385 show named vessels shipping quantities of cloth of various kinds: 'white stretched', 'russet', 'kersey', 'broad', 'blanket' and 'Galeys' (Welsh flannel). In addition to this, Dartmoor continued to be a source of tin, and the local fishing grounds were sufficiently rich as to provide for exports of dried fish – this latter trade requiring vessels for both the harvesting and the export of the product. A ledger from the same time shows white herrings, hake and 'Brodefysshe' (perhaps skate or ray) being loaded at Dartmouth in substantial quantities and in 1379, we see ingots of tin and iron coming under the scrutiny of the customs officials.[23] In all, however, it seems likely that Dartmouth was more important for its imports than its exports and more important for its shipping than for any principal trading activity. Its excellent natural harbour provided a convenient place for goods to be transhipped, but the difficulty of overland transport and its distance from any larger centre of population made it of little value as a final destination.

However, the obverse of the geographical handicap which Dartmouth bore in relation to the wool trade across the Narrow Sea was its advantageous position in relation to the ports of Gascony, through which flowed England's huge imports of wine. There is no doubt that the first phase of the emergence of Dartmouth as a specialist port coincided with the growth of the Gascon wine trade, and the way in which this trade changed and contracted with the outbreak of the Hundred Years War also explains much about the way in which the focus of its activity later shifted from principal trading to privateering.

For the first thirty-five years of the fourteenth century, the wine trade was stable and prosperous. In the first years of Edward III's reign, up to one hundred thousand tuns of wine were shipped from Bordeaux and the neighbouring Gironde port of Libourne. Of this, it is estimated that between a fifth and a quarter were exported to England[24] and, after 1330, most of this trade came, for the first time, into the hands of English rather than Gascon merchants. It is likely, therefore, that the heyday of Dartmouth's Bordeaux wine trade was seen in the early 1330s. The outbreak of the war, however, posed an immediate threat to both the vineyards and to the ships carrying the wine. Between 1337 and 1340, there was almost constant fighting in the wine producing regions of Gascony, starting in the Agenais and eventually enveloping the Bordelais itself. Wine shipments out of Bordeaux naturally plummeted and the supply of quality wines from the Haut Pays declined by around ninety percent. This was a pattern which was to become established and, although the trade stabilised somewhat in the truce of the 1340s, from then onwards the bulk of shipments came from the closer environs of Bordeaux.

There was a modest recovery in shipments before 1340 and this can be attributed to the measures which were taken to protect the wine when it was at sea. Whereas ships carrying wine had before the war sailed more or less continuously from early October to late spring, the enforcement of a convoy system meant that shipments became concentrated into shorter periods and prices, accordingly, fluctuated wildly. Such was the value of the cargo that ships which had been arrested for the king's service were sometimes released to join the wine convoys. Also, as the threat of attack was now constant, the ships had to be capable of protecting themselves. Increased manning levels – sometimes two or even three times the pre-war numbers – and the logistical problems surrounding the assembly of convoys also substantially increased shipment costs. And it was not only ships plying the long route from Bordeaux to the Western Approaches that were under threat. Until Edward's victory at Sluys, the whole of the south coast of England was under more or less constant naval threat and such was the level of insecurity at sea that in 1339 wine was transported by road from Bristol to London, over roads so bad that the carts often overturned, resulting in the breaching of barrels and the loss of their precious contents.[25]

The truce of 1340, which endured for five years, brought imports and prices back to pre-war levels but it is likely that England, and English merchants were, by this time, just taking a larger share of a sharply diminished Bordeaux trade. Although the Agenais and some of the other formerly wine-producing regions outside the Bordelais were retaken after hostilities recommenced in 1345, their vineyards had been devastated in the fighting. Wine imports into England were to remain at a low level for fifteen years and plumbed the depths when the Black Death overtook the Bordelais in early 1348. Wine was to become a scarcer and more precious commodity

The merchant shipowners of Dartmouth continued to be prominently involved in the diminished, more hazardous trade for the rest of the century and beyond, but the character of the trade, and of those involved in it, underwent a profound change from the 1340s onwards. When the wine fleet of 1372 sailed for the Gironde, it was in need of substantially increased protection. The crew of one of the convoy vessels, the *Katrine* of Dartmouth, was increased from her normal complement of twenty-six to fifty, implying that she was carrying twenty-four men whose sole purpose was to fight. She was, in effect, converted into a naval vessel ballasted with wine.

Dartmouth had emerged as an important port because of its position close to a major route of peaceful commerce. The wine that had flowed plentifully and relatively cheaply to Hawley's Hoe and the town's other quays before the outbreak of the war was now a treasure to be guarded and to be fought over. The Dartmouth men were still placed close to the action and wine was to continue to feature prominently in their working lives. The critical difference was that, whereas the first John Hawley could trade peaceably in the products of Bordeaux, his son and grandson were to become accustomed to acquiring them by force.

Chapter Three:

The Shipmen

Shipmen and Ships

Chaucer's cameo description of the Shipman suggests that the poet had quite a clear understanding of the world which the late medieval mariner inhabited. He alludes to the hostile and difficult environment in which such men lived and worked and the skills and traits necessary to cope with it. The men who went to sea during the lives of Chaucer and Hawley did so using technologies that had changed little for thousands of years. European civilisation was on the brink of scientific discoveries and technical innovations which were to have a profound influence on maritime practice, but these were still in the future.

Seamanship is a discipline which has developed over the centuries in an accretive manner, as generations of sailors have applied extraordinary ingenuity to imposing their will on an environment whose multi-faceted vagaries defy orderly analysis. This was based at first on simple observations of natural phenomena, such as the movement of tides, the positions and movements of celestial bodies and the direction and strength of the wind. Where patterns could be discerned, they were learnt and the knowledge thus acquired was sometimes used to make predictions on the basis of which voyages and other maritime activities could be planned. Finally, astronomy and the other relevant sciences provided precise descriptions of not only the working of these phenomena but of how and why they work as they do, greatly improving the tools available to mariners. This was a process which accelerated over time but it had barely begun when Hawley sailed.

Hawley's sailors were coast-huggers and rock-dodgers. They had no very useful navigation instruments, no hydrographical or tidal charts or tables of much worth and no weather forecasts beyond what they could see by looking to windward or could guess from experience. Sailors who seldom ventured far from shore often used depth soundings to ascertain their positions. For this they used lead weights with tallow attached to the bottom, with which they could retrieve samples of the seabed material – local knowledge did the rest. Chaucer's veteran seaman used rules of thumb and sailed 'view to view '. He knew "*His stremes, and his daungers hym bisides, His herberwe and his moone, his lodemenage*"; he also "*knew alle the havenes as they were, From Gootlond to the Cape of Fynystere, and every cryke in Britaigne and in Spayne*". He knew that tidal ranges and strengths varied considerably with the season and the phases of the moon, sometimes aiding and sometimes hindering docking and other manoeuvres. He knew from experience and from rudimentary tide tables when the tides would change and how high or strong they would probably be[*]. But that was all he knew; experience was everything.

The tide in Start Bay runs firmly to the south and west for two hours after low tide at Dartmouth. It then slackens and reverses direction. When the masters of Hawley's ships sailed for St Mathieu in the 1380s they would have known this. They would also have known that if the wind was blowing strongly from the south or south-west, they would be better advised to delay their departure. To do otherwise would be a waste of time and precious supplies and would hazard their ships unnecessarily. If, on the other hand, the wind had started to blow steadily from the north or north-east, they would hurry to warp out into the middle of the Dart and sail on the end of the strong ebb tide from the estuary, picking up the favourable tidal stream in the bay and, cramming on sail, they would clear Start Point and head for France. If, as night fell, the sky was clear, they would sail with the Pole Star at such an angle off the ship's starboard quarter as to put them on course for a landfall somewhere at the western end of the north coast of Brittany. In perfect conditions they might make a perfect crossing and a perfect landfall in perhaps twenty-two hours. From three miles or so offshore, their unaided eyes would identify some rock, island or landmark, telling them that they had reached a known part of the coastline, and they could then adjust their course to work due southwards towards Le Conquet, perhaps confirming their position by spotting the Île de Molène on the horizon off their starboard beam.

The crossing thus described would have been luxuriously straightforward and would have tested the master's skills hardly at all[†]. If, however, the sky was overcast, the sea rough and the wind direction variable, things would be very different. The

---

[*] *The terms 'spring' for tides where the tidal range is large and 'neap' where it is small, are old English words, with which medieval mariners would be familiar, meaning 'jump' and 'low'. Although the largest tidal ranges of the year occur with the equinoctial new and full moons, 'spring' has nothing to do with the season.*

[†] *Watkin cites the fourteenth century chronicler, Thomas Walsingham, stating that the fleet of Edward I, having been forced by adverse winds into 'Dortemutham', left the port on October 8th 1294 and arrived at St Mathieu on the morning of October 10th. This perhaps reflects a more normal time of 36–48 hours for this crossing. (Watkin p.354)*

helmsman may have had a simple magnetic compass needle, whose wild swings he might read from experience to give him a reasonable idea of his heading. He could also use simple, home-made charts and dead reckoning, using hour glasses and estimates of his speed, perhaps using a crude log*. But he would never know his position with any confidence unless he could see some landmark and, when barrelling downwind in the dark or in murky weather, the proximity required for any landmark to be visible might mean that the ship, unable to claw off a lee shore, would be placed in immediate peril. In anything but perfect conditions, any kind of voyage across the open sea involved known dangers and required a significant degree of skill.

These were, however, skills which seamen had possessed for generations and, while even the comparatively short sea crossings which were made by Hawley's ships were still hazardous, they were able to cope with the hazards with a near-routine facility. Simple compasses were quite widely used by the late fourteenth century but some mariners managed without them and the more advanced tools and techniques of navigation were a necessary product of an age of trans-oceanic voyages which was yet to come. The seamen of Genoa and other Mediterranean ports were beginning to experiment with more advanced techniques but the English mariners of the late Middle Ages still depended primarily on their memory and judgement. They were coast-huggers and rock-dodgers but they hugged and dodged with some skill and their simple navigational techniques were, for the most part, sufficient for their needs.

The development of ship design proceeded along a similar intellectual path to that of navigation. Sailors had no concept of the aerodynamics of sails or of the hydrodynamics of keels or rudders, but they knew, by trial and error, what worked and what did not and, as new demands were made on them, they adapted known structures and techniques to suit. Ship design has always involved compromises and the different types of vessels used in Hawley's time had evolved to serve specific purposes in specific conditions. The nomenclature of medieval ship designs is complex and often inconsistent. One scholar has compiled a census of English vessels mentioned in accounts of the early period of the Hundred Years War, finding: one 'buss', two 'flunes', two 'galiots', two 'hulks', three 'doggers', three 'lodships', five 'crayers', five 'spinaces', six 'galleys', seven 'carracks', twelve 'barges', twelve 'nefs', thirteen 'tarites', nineteen 'boats', forty-six 'ships', and one hundred and eighty-seven 'cogs'[26]. Elsewhere we find mention of 'navis', 'batell', 'trygo' and 'scapho'. Different types of sailing vessels in later centuries were often defined by reference to technical characteristics which would be meaningless to the layman and, even today, relatively close scrutiny is required to distinguish, for example, a ketch from a yawl, but the definitions have at least become specific and consistent. This was less true in the Middle Ages, when different terms might be applied to the same vessel.

The more sophisticated 'chip log', attached to the knotted rope from which the name for speed units at sea derives, did not appear until the sixteenth century.

For the purpose of our story, however, the task of defining and describing the vessels involved is relatively straightforward. This is because, although larger vessels were beginning to appear in the early fifteenth century and although *tarites, carracks* and other esoteric Mediterranean types put in occasional appearances in our story, most of the action involves galleys, crayers, barges, balingers and cogs.

The galley was the only specialist type of warship which operated in the Channel in the late Middle Ages. Galleys were long and narrow and carried very large crews. They had sails to provide auxiliary propulsion but sailed very poorly and their defining characteristic and single tactical advantage was in their banks of oars, pulled by oarsmen sitting on rows of benches. Although the galley was a Mediterranean invention and was little suited to the conditions of the Atlantic seas, it was operated to considerable effect by some of the Atlantic states, notably the kingdom of Castile, which used it in the inhospitable Bay of Biscay. Their comparatively narrow beam and the limitations placed on freeboard by the necessity of putting the oars into the water, however, made galleys susceptible to swamping in heavy seas and their large manning ratios and limited accommodation put severe constraints on their operating range. The French built and maintained galley fleets in the fourteenth century, importing shipwrights from Genoa to the royal shipyards in Normandy. Galleys were never, however, adopted with any enthusiasm in England.

The small, single-masted, barge-like crayer was the workhorse of coastal trade on both sides of the Channel. Designed to maximise carrying capacity, which ranged from ten to sixty or seventy tons, crayers were slow and unwieldy. Although their crews might sometimes put up a spirited defence if attacked, they were never used in aggressive actions and appear throughout the story of John Hawley's maritime operations in the role of more or less easy victims of privateers.

The balinger, an important vessel in the life of Hawley, is more resistant to precise definition. It is possible that balingers had their origins in the whaling boats used on the Breton and Biscay coasts but they evolved and grew in size over time. They clearly started as craft which could be propelled by oars over some distance, although they were primarily sailing vessels and the design evolved, growing in size over the years and eventually, in the latter part of the fifteenth century, carrying a hundred tons or more and sometimes having two masts. In Hawley's time, they were invariably single-masted and would typically carry twenty to fifty tuns, although some were much larger. Being flush-decked, they were comparatively fast and agile.

Except where the word 'barge' is specifically used to refer to royal barges or to transport barges in the more modern sense, its precise medieval meaning is difficult to discern, the vessels referred to being difficult to distinguish from balingers. It is possible that it was used as a generic word to refer to small cogs or to flush-decked vessels with auxiliary oar propulsion. Chaucer may, therefore, have had a balinger or cog in mind when he conjured up the "*barge*" that was "*y-clept*" the

"*Maudelayne*". Hawley certainly owned a number of balingers/barges over the years and these are specifically referred to as such in surviving records but his legend is associated most closely with the largest and most imposing vessel which was common in England at that time – the cog.

The cog was the archetypal large sailing vessel in northern European waters in the late Middle Ages. Its image appears on seals, coats of arms and illuminated manuscripts throughout the period and, while its originally intended purpose was as the workhorse of the deep-water merchant fleet, it is

The lateen rig had some advantages over square sails but the huge yards were judged too difficult to handle in stormy northern waters.

Illustration from Encyclopaedia Britannica 1911

usually the round-hulled, single-masted cog, with its raised poop and forecastle and a fighting top fitted above the yard of its single, square sail, which is at the centre of the action where sea battles are illustrated in contemporary chronicles.

All of Hawley's vessels, and the great majority of those which their crews would encounter at sea, were single-masted and square-rigged. Although additional masts offered greatly improved manoeuvrability, particularly in larger vessels, and more complex 'divisible' sail plans improved sailing performance, they were not widely adopted in England until long after Hawley's death. The single, loose-footed square sail, bent onto a symmetrical, horizontal yard had some advantages, particularly in stability and comparative ease of handling, and its area could be reduced by lowering the yard and partially furling the canvas using reefing lines, as the wind speed increased. The area of the standard working sail would be chosen to optimise performance in most conditions but, if additional area was required, this could be achieved by lacing additional panels, known as 'bonnets' to the sail's foot*. This sail plan was, however, considerably less efficient in some respects than were the various types of lateen rig which were common in the Mediterranean at the time. Lateen rigs, which probably had their origins in the Arab dhows of the Red Sea, had asymmetrical, triangular sails attached to long, asymmetrical balance lugsail yards, which gave stability to the luff, or leading edge, of the sail, allowing the vessel to sail much closer to the wind than was possible with double-luffed, square sail, although they did sail significantly better on one tack than the other because the sail inevitably pressed against the mast when close-hauled on the 'bad' tack. It is generally thought that these were not

---

* *Not to be confused with the spritsail of the same name used by later ships.*

adopted in northern waters because the more hostile sea and weather conditions made the long, heavy lateen yards difficult and dangerous to handle.

The square sail plan was essentially unchanged from that used in ancient times, but there had been some advances in hull designs in the later Middle Ages. The most important of these was the introduction of the rudder hung on a vertical or near-vertical sternpost, with a tiller attached at an oblique angle to it. This superseded the much less efficient steering oar which had been used previously and was still quite common. Another, probably accidental, innovation was the stem post. The round-hulled ships of the time were designed to maximise carrying capacity at the inevitable expense of sailing qualities and were generally bluff-bowed, but the use of a narrow stem post which extended up the ship's bow provided a cutwater, however much the vessel pitched in the waves, and improved the flow of the water past the hull, increasing speed and improving the ability to point into the wind.

Marine archaeologists have discovered the remains of very few ships from this period and knowledge of crayers, balingers and the like remains sketchy, but one precious discovery has greatly enhanced our understanding of the cog. During dredging work in the River Weser in the port of Bremen in 1962 the remains of a cog were found in the mud. Dendrochronological analysis of its timbers indicated that the oak trees used in the timbers of the ship's hull were felled in the autumn of 1378 and that she was built in 1380. She had been under construction and near completion when she was washed down the river as a result of a storm or tidal event but, had she ever sailed, she would have been an exact contemporary of the vessels operated by John Hawley when he was in his forties and fifties.*

The Bremen cog was a Hanseatic trading vessel and not of English origin, but there is every reason to believe that she was very similar in design and construction to the cogs used by Hawley and approximately of an average size. She had an overall length of seventy-six feet, was fifty-nine feet long at the waterline, and had a beam of nearly twenty-four feet. The clinker-built hull was round-bilged and nearly flat-bottomed, being caulked using moss, animal hair and tar. She drew seven feet five inches; her hull weight was fifty-two tons; she displaced ninety-two tons when sailing in ballast and one hundred and twenty-eight tons fully laden. Her cargo capacity is thus estimated at around seventy-six tons. Although she lacked the raised forecastle of many cogs of the time, she had an aftercastle which rose more than fourteen feet above the waterline. There were two wooden windlasses – one for raising and lowering the anchor and one for general use on the aftercastle. It is thought that the deck planks would have leaked significantly in a heavy sea and that conditions below would therefore have been very wet. The cargo could only have been kept dry by using barrels and other watertight containers. There is also evidence that some kind of bilge

---

* *The painstakingly reconstructed and preserved Hanse Cog is on display at the German Maritime Museum in Bremerhaven.*

*The Hanse Cog replica close reaching
– Note the extremely long yard.*

Copyright c 2000-2001 Jan Maat

www.janmaat.de/kogge.htm

pump had been installed. The ship had a high bulwark which would have afforded some limited shelter to the crew, who would have been required to spend their days and nights on deck. It would also have provided some protection if the ship were involved in a battle, while the helmsman was sheltered from the elements – and from enemy missiles – under the aftercastle. This latter arrangement had the disadvantage that the helmsman was unable to see what was immediately ahead and needed to be guided by instructions from the deck for close manoeuvring.

What makes the Bremen discovery particularly informative is that the archaeologists not only pieced the original ship back together from thousands of fragments; they also built an exact replica, the *Ubena von Bremen*, using the same materials and even incorporated some asymmetries in the hull which were present in the original. The replica has been sailed extensively and its sailing qualities have been the subject of very detailed analysis. The original rudder and rig, if they were ever made, were not found and those of the replica were designed on the basis of medieval images and modern calculations. Whether the replica rig and steering gear, designed by twentieth-century German marine architects, are more or less efficient than the original, which was made using the experience and rules of thumb of their late medieval forebears, we do not know.

The German scientists found that a crew of fourteen was required just to handle the ship and even a cursory examination of the rig makes it easy to understand why such a large crew would be necessary to handle a simple ship of such a modest size. The replica carries a mainsail of one thousand three hundred and eighty square feet and one or two bonnets, each of three hundred and forty square feet. The sail is bent onto a yard which is forty-eight feet long, suspended sixty feet above the deck on a seventy-eight foot mast. Even given her high freeboard, the German crew found that she could not be allowed to heel by more than twelve to fifteen degrees, as she risked being swamped if these angles were exceeded in heavy seas. In order to reef the sail, the yard must be lowered and the heavy canvas partly brailed up with the reefing lines[†]. In a choppy sea and a rising wind, handling such a large and

---

[*] *Reduce sail area*

[†] *In the 13th-15th centuries, reef points were attached to the lower part of the sail. The sail was therefore furled from the bottom. The reefing lines were, in later times, attached to the sail in rows below the yard and the sail was brailed up to the yard progressively from the top – giving a more efficient shape.*

heavy sail and yard in a restricted space demands a good deal of muscle power and is potentially very dangerous. It is easy to see why lateen rigs, with their even longer yards, never caught on among sailors who operated in stormy northern waters.

The sailing performance of the Bremen replica cog gives us some insights into the constraints which the weather and wind direction would have placed on the operations of Hawley's crews. The speeds which the ship achieved during tests when reaching and sailing downwind were quite respectable. Sailing on a broad reach in a near gale (force seven on the Beaufort scale) she briefly achieved speeds of eight knots but, unlike vessels with more modern rigs, was consistently fastest when travelling directly downwind. In the Beaufort force four or five winds that might be considered typical in the Channel and the Western Approaches, she turned in average speeds of four or five knots over all courses. The maximum downwind speed of any sailing vessel which sails in displacement is determined by its waterline length and, in this sense, the performance of the cog compares reasonably with other sailing cargo vessels and even with some modern cruising yachts.

The cog's Achilles heel, however, was a near-complete inability to sail upwind. This weakness was common to square-rigged ships throughout the age of sail but there is little doubt that the cogs were particularly unhandy in this respect. Under full sail, in light winds and in sheltered waters, the replica cog was capable of sailing at an angle of approximately seventy degrees to the wind but made significant leeway (i.e. drifted sideways) when doing so, which means that her effective tacking angle was not much better than a hundred and eighty degrees. When reefed, in stronger winds or in the open sea, the inefficient hull and sail plan and the extensive top-hamper meant that the ship was unable to make any way upwind at all and, in fact, lost ground. What this means in practice is that, while the fastest modern racing yachts, with their highly efficient, fore-and-aft rigs, can sail anywhere through approximately three hundred degrees of the compass, the cogs, even in ideal conditions, could sail in less than two hundred degrees.

The prevailing wind across south-west England and the Western Approaches blows broadly from the south-west. The wind roses for Plymouth and Brest suggest that Hawley's cogs, given this weakness in their sailing properties, could have made the perfect crossing from Dartmouth to Brittany described above on maybe one day in ten and would have struggled to make any progress at all towards their destination on four days in ten. The return journey, of course, would have been conversely easy for four days in ten but there would have been times when unfavourable winds pinned them down in port – at either end of their journey – for weeks on end*.

The difficulties faced by the mariners who routinely undertook the upwind slog to the west receive a passing mention in an entry in the Patent Rolls for January 1449, a reference which testifies to the advantage of Dartmouth's westerly location:

The inability of ships to make way upwind sometimes changed the course of history. Edward III planned to take his army to Gascony, not Normandy, in 1346. If the wind had served for Gascony, the Battle of Crécy would never have taken place.

"Whereas Neuport in the Isle of Wight is situated on the sea, where many masters and mariners of ships winter in their passage to Aquitaine and Bordeaux in quest of wines and other merchandise, for safety, until a strong wind rise for their voyage…"[27]

The cog was designed to carry large barrels and other cargo. The vessel's tonnage derived from the number of tuns*, usually of wine, that it could carry but it was constantly being remodelled to serve other purposes. Cogs were often used to carry military stores and troops, and were frequently modified to provide accommodation for horses and means of embarking and disembarking them. They were favoured as fighting vessels because their raised fore- and after-castles provided lofty platforms for the archers and spearmen to fight from. Small platforms were also attached to their masts, above their mainsail yards, to be used as fighting tops. Their bulk and extensive freeboard also enabled them to run down smaller craft, but it should be noted that a cog arrayed for war, with the additional windage and top-hamper created by such modifications, probably sailed even more poorly upwind than one configured for merchant service.

Whatever its shortcomings, the versatility of this 'round ship' caused it to become, in the latter half of the fourteenth century, the predominant type of deep-water vessel used for both mercantile and naval purposes. Cogs carried anything and everything. Those used by Hanseatic merchants exported, among other things, surplus wheat and rye from Poland, timber, pitch and other forestry products from Russia and Poland and herrings from Sweden. On their return voyages to the Baltic, they shipped salt from Brittany and cloth from Flanders. The pattern of trade for the cogs of Dartmouth and other Devon ports was very different. The cargo whose shipment had been the original *raison d'être* of Dartmouth as a significant port was Gascon wine and the sheer quantities to be transported had caused ever larger cogs to be built. In the thirteenth century, cogs of a hundred tons or more were unusual; by the early fourteenth century there were ships operating in the Anglo-Gascon wine trade which displaced two hundred or even three hundred tons[28].

The apogee of the Gascon wine trade marked the end of the first phase of the development of Dartmouth as a specialist port. Wine was never the sole commodity to be imported there and wool and woollen cloth were never its sole exports. Dartmouth traded in small quantities of tin, lead, iron, dried fish, bow staves and most of the other requisites of commercial and military life, but this miscellaneous commerce never added up to enough to justify the substantial maritime infrastructure that had been put in place and it was perhaps inevitable that, when the outbreak of the Hundred Years War disrupted the wine and wool trades, the shipowners of the town would start to employ their balingers and cogs for more warlike purposes.

---

* *A tun was equal to two pipes, four hogsheads or 252 gallons.*

The cogs and balingers of the merchant shipmen performed a variety of roles in support of military action, mainly auxiliary and logistical, but the balance of their activities changed as the Hundred Years War progressed, becoming steadily more offensive and warlike. Ships were increasingly used in raids on enemy coasts and on shipping. Both the role and the form of the ships evolved gradually. England possessed no purpose-built warships until well after Hawley's death, but a cog 'arrayed for war' might be regarded as a warship for all practical purposes, although the only structural concession to this specialist role could be seen in the raised forecastles and fighting tops which were added to the basic cog design. Even these were often *ad hoc* and temporary modifications.

The navy, such as it was, was just an army afloat; and sea warfare was, for the most part, an extension of land warfare. The ships of Hawley's time seldom carried guns and, when they did, they were small, extremely inaccurate and often as much a hazard to their operators as to the enemy. Nor did mariners have telescopes or any well-developed means of signalling and the days when squadrons of ships could effectively patrol large areas of sea, communicating with one another at a distance of several miles, were still far in the future. This, combined with the slowness and inability of vessels to make much way upwind, meant that interception in the open sea, on the rare occasions when it happened, was an essentially fortuitous event. Ships were captured when close to shore or, very often, while in port and the typical objective was to draw alongside an enemy vessel and overwhelm its crew in much the same way as on land.

Sailing tactics would sometimes have a bearing on the outcome of a fight and any skipper who held the weather gage*, as always in the age of sail, had the advantage of speed and manoeuvrability and could often choose whether to fight or retire. It is also the case that fireships and other devices specific to maritime warfare were sometimes used, but the evolution of the specialised tools and techniques of naval warfare was at a very early stage. Fireships apart, there was little in the way of specialised maritime weaponry. Stone-throwing was perhaps more prevalent in sea battles than on land and contemporary drawings show large stones being thrown from fighting tops onto the decks of enemy ships. Crude catapults of one kind and another were also used to throw stones, with rocky beaches presumably providing an inexhaustible source of ammunition.

Vessels could be rammed and sunk; they could be burned by fireships or, in some cases, by flaming projectiles. They could be disabled by having their halyards or other rigging cut but, for the most part, it was not the fabric of the ship but the crew and the soldiers aboard at which the weapons were aimed. When two or more vessels came together and battle was joined, swords, spears and other such weapons were employed hand-to-hand by the lightly armoured

---

* *i.e. was significantly upwind of his opponent.*

troops on board. The super weapon of the day, however, at sea as well as on land, and so ubiquitous that it seldom warranted mention in accounts of sea fights, was the English longbow.

Although it had its origins in Wales, it was the English yeomanry who developed the longbow, endlessly trained with it and made it their own. It was a delicate weapon whose apparent simplicity was underlain by a sophisticated structure. Bow staves were carefully cut from the point at which the heartwood of yews, ash and other suitable trees*, met the sapwood. The stave would be rough-hewn into a D-section consisting of two layers – the heartwood on the inner, rounded side and the sapwood on the outer, flat face. The heartwood was resistant to compression, while the sapwood performed well in tension. This meant that the natural elasticity of the stave was asymmetrical; it built up a powerful reflexive energy when bent one way. The bowyer or archer dried the stave for up to two years and gradually shaped it in a way which took advantage of this one-way elasticity and adjusted its length and thickness to suit the archer's height and upper body strength. The whole process could take up to four years. The result was a bow which was usually around six feet in length with a draw force of sixty to a hundred pounds. An exceptionally strong bowman could pull one hundred and fifty pounds or more. In order to cope with this power, the English hemp bowstrings were about four millimetres thick[†]. These were produced by specialists and were often supplied with a back-spliced loop at one end and were cut to a suitable length by the archer. Spare strings were invariably carried into battle, often coiled up in the archers' hats. The length of the arrows used depended on the length of the archer's arm, extending from the knuckle of his bow hand to the cheek to which he drew the string. This was typically around thirty-one inches or one 'cloth-yard', and the arrow's length and columnar strength endowed it with considerable penetrative force. Arrows were usually fletched with goose or peacock feathers, carefully trimmed for optimum range and directional stability, and had barbed steel points, some of the heavier ones being fitted with massive, square 'bodkin' points able to penetrate chain mail and even plate armour. A typical quiver would consist of eight light, long-range 'flight' arrows, weighing two ounces or so, and sixteen heavier arrows, of three to four ounces, for close-range fighting. A bowman would take two or three quivers with him into battle.

The longbow was the decisive weapon in battles throughout most of the Hundred Years War and the tactical skill with which it was deployed at Agincourt was instrumental in what was, against all odds, arguably the most astonishing and

---

* *Some bows were, as legend would have it, made of English yew but it was usually too contorted and knotty to be of any use. Yew staves were imported; mainly from Spain and Italy. In order to maintain supplies, wine importers were obligated to import a quota of bow staves with each consignment of their merchandise.*

† *Although few medieval bowstrings or arrows have survived, this estimate is confirmed by the width of the niche in the bone arrow nocks which have.*

total victory in English military history. As a result, a considerable romantic folklore has grown up around the exploits of medieval English bowmen and extravagant claims are sometimes made for the accuracy and power of their shooting. Although it is said that the skill of the archers was such that they could aim for gaps in an enemy's armour and that a French knight in battle would open his visor at his peril, this degree of skill and composure was probably rare. While a high degree of accuracy could be achieved at close quarters, much of the damage was done by the archers aiming at a general area and discharging volleys of arrows at high speed and at a range of up to two hundred and fifty yards. An experienced bowman, on solid ground, could loose an aimed arrow every three seconds or so and a group of any size could thus take a heavy, if largely indiscriminate, toll, showering an intimidating barrage of arrows and inflicting terrible wounds on the men and animals in the target area. Once his arrows were exhausted, in perhaps five minutes or less, the archer became a foot soldier, drawing his sword and fighting hand-to-hand in the general mêlée.

We might imagine that the shipboard archer, perched on a fighting top, hampered by rigging or other obstructions and unable to place the arrows within easy reach, point-down, into the ground in front of him, might shoot less quickly but, on the other hand, he would never be confronted with a cavalry charge and could better afford to take his time. Although the crossbow, which was easy to aim and whose bolts traced a flat trajectory, might have been somewhat better suited for shipboard use than for the wider chaos of the battlefield, the French crossbowmen, ashore or afloat, were generally no match for the English archers*, whose skills were a result of prolonged and incessant training and practice. Longbow archery was a skill which took years to perfect and the English kings invested heavily in the critical military advantage which it conferred[†]. This can be seen in the huge numbers in which archers were employed, both on land and at sea, throughout the period. As early as 1317, four vessels manned by forty-two men-at-arms and ninety-nine archers were patrolling the sea between Edinburgh and Berwick on behalf of Edward II[29], and, in 1420 we see the younger John Hawley sailing to serve Henry V with a personal force of fifty men-at-arms and one hundred archers. The yeoman archers consistently outnumbered the men-at-arms by two to one.

Archers and men-at-arms were used in this ratio and to notable effect in one of the very few large, set-piece sea battles to take place during the Hundred Years War – the Battle of Sluys. This, the best-documented large sea fight of the whole period, took

---

* *The French eventually realised the importance of the longbow and started to use it themselves but never to any strategic effect.*

† *Archery practice was made compulsory and Edward III famously banned football and other games in 1363, in order that the yeomanry should not be distracted by such frivolity.*

place in 1340, the year in which it is generally supposed that John Hawley was born. It cannot in any way be regarded as a typical naval action of the time, but it does provide an insight into the tactics used and the way in which sea battles were joined and, as such, aids our understanding of the smaller, scrappier engagements which were more typical and in which Hawley's men were so often involved. It is also illustrative of the brutal rules under which the war at sea was waged throughout his lifetime.

The battle took place in front of the town of Sluys, on a stretch of water which no longer exists. Extensive silting and land reclamation has transformed the shape of that low-lying area of Flanders and the modern Dutch town (Sluis) lies some four miles inland. The events which led up to the battle were complex and, for the kingdom of Edward III, perilous. French, Castilian and Genoese galleys had been roaming the Channel, virtually unchallenged, since the spring of 1338, had taken Guernsey and had sacked a number of towns along the south coast of England, including Southampton. Five English ships, including one of Edward's largest, the cog *Christopher*, had been taken in harbour at Arnemuiden and this latter vessel was now deployed against him as part of a large force under the Monegasque Carlo Grimaldi.[30]

By the end of 1339, however, Grimaldi's galleys had returned to Monaco[*] and a somewhat disorganised English fleet under Lord Morley, Admiral of the North and East, was able to mount counterattacks on the French coast. In 1340, Edward signalled a more general offensive and, on June 22nd, sailed from the Orwell aboard his cog *Thomas*, with a force which numbered, according to the varying estimates of the chroniclers of the time, 120-160 sail. He made a fast crossing and was in sight of the entrance to the River Zwin, off Sluys, the following day. There he encountered the Franco-Castilian-Genoese fleet of between two and three hundred vessels, bound together in a defensive formation of three lines, at anchor in the mouth of the estuary. Contemporary accounts of the battle are confusing but agree on one crucial point – that Edward's fleet attacked the following day with the sun behind them – implying that they either they had waited until very late in that midsummer day in order to achieve this, or had outflanked the defensive formation by making their approach from the Western Scheldt to the east, risking grounding on the treacherous shoals between.

It appears that Edward sent his ships into the attack in groups of three, with two manned almost entirely by archers and one with men-at-arms. As the panicked enemy broke formation, their ships were picked off individually, being softened up, ahead of boarding by the men-at-arms, by the archers raining arrows down on them. This tactic seems to have established a crucial early advantage and, although the battle raged into the night, an English victory was assured. The defeated troops, with nowhere to retreat to, were killed on

---

[*] *Philip VI had a rather vexed relationship with the mercenary galley commanders and the larger fleet of Ayton Doria had also returned to its home port of Genoa, after a disagreement over pay.*

the decks of their ships or thrown overboard where, usually encumbered and weighed down by armour, they mostly drowned. It seems that, where Edward III fought and had the upper hand, like Chaucer's Shipman, *"By water he sente hem hoom to every lond."*

Sluys was a victory at which the cog *Christopher* and some measure of English confidence were recaptured and it certainly averted any immediate threat of invasion, but it did not give Edward control of the sea. He and his successors were to struggle to achieve that for decades to come and their continuing inability to do so gave rise to a class of maritime opportunist of which John Hawley was to become an outstanding example. The cog and the longbow were the most important tools of his trade.

Sailors of Fortune

Military service had for centuries been a central pillar of the feudal system and, while feudalism in its purest form no longer ordered the lives of the English during the hundred years or so when the Hawleys lived in Dartmouth, its well-established contractual relationships still functioned routinely when soldiers were required in order to fight the enemies of the king. The military command structure mirrored the broader social system and it was through the chivalric hierarchy that the necessary troops were mustered in times of conflict.

During prolonged periods of warfare there were, in effect, standing armies but their mustering and armament was always organised at a more local level and payments were made to the various classes of soldiers according to their status, and also in respect of the equipment which they provided. The feudal levy, as such, had long since ceased to be the means by which armies were raised and the relationship between the granting of knightly estates and the obligation of military service had been much diluted. Even those most highly placed in the social order, including the Black Prince[*] himself, drew their pay at fixed daily rates and the costs of warfare therefore were borne substantially by the central exchequer. A knight and his esquires and the yeoman archers were, however, awarded the fixed rates of pay only if they presented themselves properly equipped and if they and their equipment – down to the last horseshoe, arrow and bowstring – passed muster. This mercenary arrangement implicitly recognised that military equipment was expensive and that it would be impossible to raise a functional army unless the system of payment reflected not only the basic victualling requirements of the troops but also the cost of their weaponry and specialist gear. The matching of the payments made to the costs incurred was never perfect and a knight might emerge from a campaign having made a profit or a loss from the exercise. The system was, however, designed to minimise that risk.

---

[*] *The first-born son of Edward III, Edward of Woodstock, Prince of Wales, acted as regent when his father was campaigning abroad. Like his father, he was an enthusiastic soldier. He was never referred to as the Black Prince during his lifetime, that now-universal appellation having been a much later creation of historians.*

The Battle of Sluys was almost unique as a set-piece sea battle in this period.
From a manuscript of Froissart's Chronicles c 1470

There existed, then, something akin to a paid, professional army but England had no regular navy during the Middle Ages and there were no similar arrangements in place for those who served the king at sea. Mediterranean states such as Venice and Genoa maintained regular fleets of galleys, such as that of Carlo Grimaldi, whose specific function was to fight, but the kings of England depended almost entirely on their ability to call upon the owners of the 'round ships' of commerce in time of military need. The prevalence of a feudal tradition which failed to provide any way of financing such 'naval' needs had profound implications for the way in which medieval seamen operated and was to determine the way in which not only the careers of the Hawleys, but also the economy and life of Dartmouth, were to develop in the latter half of the fourteenth century. Nicholas Rodger puts the key point eloquently:

"Law and custom sanctioned a general duty laid on all subjects to serve the king in time of war, and no distinction was made between the knight who served with

The manner of the warfare in which the medieval kings of England engaged made the maintenance of any regular naval fleet economically impossible. When embarking troops for a campaign or *chevauchée*ˣ across the sea, they called on ships in very large numbers for transport and continuing logistical support. At other times, they had relatively little need for shipping and so a great deal of flexibility was required. The merchant shipowners were obliged to provide this flexible supply of maritime capacity but, unlike the landowning knights, whose landed possessions were granted to them partly and specifically in return for a duty of military service and whose incomes continued to flow while they were abroad and fighting on the king's behalf, they received no adequate recompense for lost income and, more particularly, loss of or damage to their ships when they were in the royal service. Thus, while the knight might receive the call to arms with some sense of foreboding, any anxieties or distaste he may have for the fight would be unrelated to the economics of the situation. The shipowner, on the other hand, stood to lose his capital and his livelihood in the event of mishap or defeat, without even a promise of chivalric glory or spectacular profit if his crews performed their tasks exceptionally well.

When fleets were assembled for specific purposes, the suitability of ships to be arrested for the royal service was largely determined by their carrying capacity and, when the king needed ships, he usually needed them in a hurry. A note of panic can perhaps be detected in the following order, issued by Henry III in pursuit of his campaign in Gascony in 1253-4, an order which also indicates that Dartmouth ships were already being arrested for the king's service well over a hundred years before John Hawley's ships were so summoned[†]:

> "To the barons and bailiffs of the ports of Hethe, Rumenal, Winchelese, Rye, Hastings, Pevenese, Sheford and Shorham. The king, while making stay in Gascony in his expedition, is in great need of his magnates of England, is therefore sending to the said ports Gilbert de London, king's clerk, to arrest all ships of the ports able to carry 16 horses, and all other like ships found there of whosoever power they be, to be at Portsmouth on the octave of Easter next, ready for the crossing of the queen, Edward, the king's son, R. earl of Cornwall, the king's brother, and other magnates coming to him in Gascony, commanding them to be aiding and counselling to the said clerk in such arrest. By like letters the king sends Roger de Evesham to the barons and bailiffs of Suhampton, Portesmuth, La Pole, Lyme, Waymue, Tengemuwe, Dertemue and Plymmue..."[32]

ˣ A campaign of general destruction and pillage, directed almost exclusively against the civilian population

† Russell (op.cit. p.31) states that Henry had called on Dartmouth ships as early as 1224 – see CPR Henry III vol.1 p.484 (in Latin).

Henry III arrested Dartmouth ships in 1224 and for his campaign in Gascony in 1253-4.

Illustration from Cassell's History of England 1902

Records of this and other expeditions such as, for example, the siege of Calais in 1346, suggest that the ships were manned, on average, by crews of twenty or so, implying that the average vessel used was of a similar size to the Bremen cog, or perhaps slightly larger. The army of Edward III at Calais is estimated to have numbered thirty-four thousand men, of whom over five thousand were knights and twenty thousand were archers – the balance being made up of squires, men-at-arms and other infantrymen. We may assume that each knight possessed at least one horse and that it would also have been necessary to transport the light horses and ponies of the hobelars and those of the archers who moved around the battlefield on horseback. Given that a vessel of seventy tons might embark sixteen horses[33], we may infer that, although the army had already been campaigning in France for some time before the siege and was therefore already in place, a substantial portion of the six hundred and ninety ships assembled for the expedition would at some point have been required to carry the horses alone.

With virtually the entire merchant fleet of southern England thus unprofitably occupied in the king's service from time to time, even the most patriotic and loyal among his shipowner subjects could perhaps be excused for taking their leave and returning to their commercial activities at the earliest possible opportunity. The implicit assumption that the shipowners were wealthy enough to bear this burden of service to the realm was perhaps justifiable in some, but certainly not all, cases. Shipowners undoubtedly were among the wealthiest of merchants and were probably the most prosperous and substantial segment of the merchant class as a whole. Their prosperity, however, depended on their ability to make very large profits on their voyages. In addition to bearing the capital cost of some of the largest assets employed by any business in the Middle Ages, the shipowners had to pay and victual large crews and would often suffer losses against which they could not insure. Gathering a substantial fleet for the royal service was very time consuming and ships were often arrested and kept inactive for extended periods. This could take shipowners to the brink of bankruptcy, as an example cited by Rodger attests:

*"In 1404 Nicholas Bygge, master of the barge Trinity of Brixham, petitioned the
crown explaining that he and his sixteen men had been under arrest for seven
weeks without pay; he had pawned all her gear to pay them, and would very soon
be ruined. A generous sovereign allowed him to visit his home port in search of
supplies but no money was offered"[34]*

Victualling costs for a long voyage, or for a voyage of unpredictable duration,
were quite substantial. A Dartmouth shipowner who was commissioned by the
king to make the long voyage to Gascony in the mid-fifteenth century shipped, in
addition to large quantities of wheat flour, four bushels of oatmeal, twenty-seven
beef carcasses, quantities of dried fish and an astonishing fifty-four pipes of beer, for
a total complement of ninety-three passengers and crew[35]. Where large numbers of
vessels congregated in preparation for expeditionary service, particularly where it
was necessary to provide food for horses as well as the men, the local provisioning
infrastructure was frequently overwhelmed.

Little is known of the normal economics of shipping during this period and
the profits earned by the shipowners would certainly have fluctuated wildly. Some
estimates put the profit margins on foreign trading voyages at as little as twenty per
cent but the figures estimated for Genoese merchants in the fourteenth century, which
indicate a return on capital of around one hundred and fifty per cent per annum[36] must
be considered to be more realistic. Economic statistics are often, however, distorted
by a 'survivor bias' and the historical record, which features the winners much more
prominently than the losers, also undoubtedly gives a misleading impression when
it portrays an invariably wealthy shipowner class. The economic risks involved in
ship-owning in northern Europe during the Hundred Years War were among the
greatest borne by any class of entrepreneur in history. The cumulative weight of
operational, meteorological and commercial risks alone would cause shipowners to
seek extraordinary returns on their successful voyages in order for the exercise to
make any kind of economic sense. Add to this the threats which any ship's master
faced at sea as a result of operating in a state of constant declared or undeclared war,
and we may readily understand why the economic imperatives of seamen differed
dramatically from those of the knights, archers and infantrymen whom they were so
often called upon to transport. Whatever hazards to life and limb they may face on
the battlefield, the knights were paid regularly and their lands provided them with
annuity incomes for life; they were thus somewhat akin to pensioned public servants.
The shipowners were risk capitalists; red in tooth and claw.

The duty of armed service borne by the landed, armigerous class provided a
relatively stable core to the armies of the English crown and this class can properly
be regarded as military. The existence of large mercenary armies of displaced
Englishmen which plagued Europe in the late Middle Ages, however, indicates
that the economic support for military action on the part of the Crown was

always precarious and that the inadequacies of the system effectively encouraged paramilitary activity and plunder, with soldiers often scavenging many miles from their line of march. The service provided by the shipowner-merchants can best be described as paranaval and, although it is clear that arrangements for suitable recompense to shipowners serving the king did evolve over time, the ability to make such payments always depended on the state of the royal coffers, which could not always be relied upon.

As the kings of England found themselves prosecuting wars simultaneously on a number of fronts, their need for maritime support increased and widened in scope. The war in France necessarily involved logistical support from the shipowners and, where the armies were unable to live off the land by plunder, constant supply and re-supply of provisions and *materiel* was required. Even the campaigns in Wales and Scotland required extensive provisioning by ship and the supply fleets tracked the progress of the armies, availing themselves of the nearest ports to the soldiers' overland routes. While it might be imagined that routine convoy work in support of a substantial army might be quite safe, this was not always the case. Grimaldi's Genoese galleys, for example, returned to capture twenty-five English supply ships during the early days of the siege of Calais and the realisation grew that, if a strong English army ran the risk of being defeated because of weaknesses in its supply train, something had to be done to protect it.

Thus, two strands of compelling logic combined to give birth to the privateer. The king needed ships to transport and supply his armies and he needed some kind of paranaval force which was capable, at the very least, of protecting his supply lines. However, if the financing of logistics and supply by sea was near-impossible, the cost of an added paranaval force to protect the whole apparatus was completely prohibitive. The inescapable conclusion was that the shipowners would simply have to finance themselves by officially sanctioned plunder. The monarchs of the island kingdom, with their continuing claims to sovereignty over lands across the sea, may have found the economics of maritime warfare particularly onerous, but the problem was shared, albeit to a lesser extent, by continental rulers, and the allure of licensed privateering as a solution was such that, by the time John Hawley took over the family business, the national and international rules of the game were well established.

Licences had been granted to privateers in England during the thirteenth century but, except where such licences were in force, captured property was considered to belong to the king. It soon became customary, however, for shipowners and crews to be entitled to the profits of their captures, except when they were specifically in the employ of the Crown at the time. Licences, or letters of marque, were then required only in specific circumstances. The international rules were quite specific and sophisticated and, although their implementation was more often than not accompanied by a degree of wrangling, their spirit was largely observed. Starting from the position that ships and goods which were the property of enemies were legitimate prizes, the rules were designed to cope with situations in which enemy ships carried goods belonging to merchants of friendly states or vice versa. If an enemy ship carrying goods belonging to non-belligerents were captured, the owners of the cargo could be invited to ransom it or, more often, when the goods were carried by the captor to his home port, they could claim restitution, bearing only the costs of freight to their chosen destination. Conversely, if a friendly or neutral ship was believed to be carrying goods belonging to an enemy, the crew might be compelled to deliver the goods to the captor's home port and would be paid the carriage costs for doing so. In reality, the arrangements were seldom as tidy as this.

The Ordinances of the Staple, enacted in 1353, gave any merchant, English or foreign, whose goods had been captured at sea, the right to reclaim them, provided that he could give evidence, either in documentary form or by his marks thereon, of his ownership. Such cases were sometimes arbitrated locally but were often referred to the admiralty courts and, where more substantial sums were involved, to the Court of Chancery. It is in the records of such tribunals that the footprints of a significant part of John Hawley's professional life are to be found.

However, although Hawley was to emerge as one of the most prominent privateers of the age, it is not in this connection that he makes his first appearance. In the last years of the reign of Edward III, Dartmouth was manifestly one of the most important ports in England. The survey cited above[37] identifies the king's ships and the home ports of other vessels in the king's service. Of the 1,291 ships identified, only thirty-one are identified as belonging to the king; the rest were arrested and, of these, Dartmouth provided seventy-one; by far the largest number from any port. Even Bristol provided only twenty-nine vessels, Southampton twenty-two, Fowey fourteen, Exmouth nine, and Plymouth just eight. When, in 1372, Edward III was once again in need of ships and naturally turned to the merchants of Dartmouth for assistance, the young John Hawley was one of that number who responded to the royal command.

Chapter Four:

The Privateer

The Rise of the Dartmouth Privateers: 1345-1377

John Hawley mounted the stage of recorded history as a man in his early thirties, fully-formed and ready to play a role which would soon bring him fame and opprobrium in almost equal measure. The suddenness of his appearance is perhaps understandable, insofar as the primary historical sources for the period consist, for the most part, of official records – of treaties, transactions, directives and disputes – and almost exclusively of the affairs of adults of some substance.

It is somewhat surprising, however, given the prominence of the local position which he was very soon to occupy, that there are no sightings of him at all when he was in his twenties. His first two appearances are as witness to conveyances of March 15th and May 10th 1372[38] but the first direct reference to him comes on September 1st of that year, in the following entry in the Borough records, which hints at the drama into which he was being drawn:

> " *Wauter Haulegh* sergeant at arms of the King and lieutenant of the Admiral gives acknowledgement by indenture to William Knoll mayor and William Stybbe bailiff of the water of Dertemouth that he had seized three ships: 'Le Margarete' owned by the said William Knoll and William Crofte, 'Le Godyer' owned by William Joke and John Gent, 'Le James' owned by John Haule and delivered them to the care of the said mayor and bailiff until the King should express his wish that they sail to Hampton where are other ships of the same port".[39]*

---

* *Not a local resident and not known to be related*

This order to arrest the vessels of Hawley and his fellow Dartmouth merchants for the king's service comes early in the second phase of the Hundred Years War. The first phase, the so-called Edwardian War, had come to a rather tentative end with the Treaty of Brétigny in 1360, which resulted from the defeat and capture of King John II of France by the forces of the Black Prince at the Battle of Poitiers in September 1356. Under the Treaty, Edward III relinquished his claim to the throne of France in return for free and clear title, without duty of homage, to lands in France which included Calais, Aquitaine and Gascony. This greatly extended England's continental holdings which, under a treaty of 1327, had been restricted to a coastal strip running from the Charente to the Pyrenees.

Given the great numerical superiority of the civilian and military populations of France at large, it was perhaps inevitable that the natural order would eventually reassert itself on the continent after the death in captivity (and consequent loss of hostage value) of John, and the ascent to the French throne of Charles V, in 1364. It took five years, but in 1369, claiming that Edward had failed to observe the terms of the Treaty of Brétigny, Charles duly declared war, initiating that phase of the conflict which is sometimes referred to as the Caroline War. This was in full swing when Hawley made his first documented appearance.

We can only assume that John Hawley came to be owner of *Le James* by 1372 as a natural consequence of his being the son of a family whose shipping business had been in existence for thirty years or so – a business of which, his father being already dead, he was now the proprietor. His subsequent behaviour and manifest business acumen suggests that he would already have enhanced the family fortune and it seems unlikely that the *James* was his only vessel. There is no record of the existence or activity of any vessel of the house of Hawley prior to this and therefore no indication of the extent to which he had been involved in shipping, principal trading, logistical support to the military or privateering, although the wealth and social standing which he had achieved suggest that he had probably been active in most or all of these. This was the period during which the demands of the war and the disruption of normal trade which it occasioned caused the Dartmouth seamen to begin their transition from peaceable traders to notorious privateers and there is a significant body of evidence concerning incidents involving other merchant mariners of the town during Hawley's childhood and youth which serve to illustrate this.

The activities of the Dartmouth privateers were controversial virtually from the outset, as they soon exhibited a tendency to ignore letters giving safe passage and even general truces, such as the one which, in theory at least, was in force from 1340-45. In April 1341, we see an order by the council at Westminster, giving:

"Commission to Gawan Corder and Roger Power, king's serjeant-at-arms, to make inquisition in the county of Devon touching a complaint by William Gascoun, merchant of Brittany, that, whereas he freighted a ship called la Katerine of the

town of Daurey with salt and other goods, at that town, some evildoers in a barge
of Dertemuth coming to the coast of Brittany, carried away the ship and cargo,
and plundered him and his fellows, mariners of the ship, of cloths and other goods,
contrary to the truces between the king and those of France, Brittany and other
lands, as he can shew by letters patent of Henry de Kere, knight, admiral of the
duke of Brittany and keeper of the coast there, to find the names of the perpetrators
of the premises, into whose hands the ship and goods have come, their value and
where they now are."[40]

The date of the incident is not stated, but the truce had been signed at Tournai
on September 25th and it may be that the Dartmouth men were already at sea by
the time news of it reached the port. A less generous interpretation, however, is
perhaps more persuasive. In any event, it is clear that, three years into the war,
they were already taking the fight to the coast of Brittany. The scale of their
operations expanded substantially after the truce and they were soon attacking
neutral shipping. Evidence of this is provided in the Patent Rolls of Edward III
for February 3rd 1346, where we see the king instructing Hervey Tyrel, Sheriff of
Devon and John Gervach, the king's sergeant at arms, to cause restitution to be
made in respect of the claim by one Sanchius Dieus, master of a Spanish ship, *la
Seinte Marie Magdaleine*, that…

"…certain malefactors of the town of Dertemuth, having fitted out and armed 13
ships of the town, whereof two belong to William Esmale of Dertemuth, boarded
the said ship freighted with 72 tuns and 1 pipe of white wine and other things and
goods of him and his fellows, merchants of Spain, with £350. while on the way to
Flanders for which part it was bound, in a place called "la Barche Dolonne" and took
away the ship and cargo, after throwing some of the mariners into the sea, and had
their will of the wines, things and goods, when they had sunk the ship…."[41]

William Smale was one of the leading burgesses of Dartmouth and was elected
mayor at Michaelmas in that same year of 1346 and, while he is not personally
named as a 'malefactor', it is implied that he would be held responsible as shipowner and explicitly stated that *"…the mayor and bailiffs of Dertemuth at their peril*
are to be obedient and attendant unto the Commissioners."
So we may infer that, at some time in 1345, a heavily manned and armed flotilla
of Dartmouth vessels, at the instigation of the town's leading burgesses and probably
led by Smale in person, was prowling the coast of France between St. Nazaire and La
Rochelle. They ambushed the hapless Spanish vessel, summarily dealt with anyone
offering resistance, sank the ship and made off with the spoils. The use of the word
'malefactor' implies simple piracy but there is no direct suggestion that those involved
should be treated as pirates. Rather, an overriding political reason is given as to why

restitution should be made in this case, that is to say that *"...inasmuch as such injuries, if not redressed, might cause a breach of the alliance with the king of Spain, just when, as the king has learned, a marriage contract between the first-born son of that king and his own daughter has been agreed on, might be occasioned, he has appointed them to investigate the matter as well by singular examinations of merchants, masters of ships, mariners and others, as by the oath of good and lawful men of the said town and other places in the county."*[42]

This refers to the betrothal of Edward's daughter, Joanna, with Pedro of Castile, a diplomatic matching which was intended to cement an alliance but which never took place, as Joanna subsequently died of the plague at Bordeaux in the summer of 1348, while travelling to Spain for the marriage. She was just fourteen.*

Whether or not the Spanish merchants were duly compensated is not a matter of record but presumably they were, while the bloodshed which had occurred was passed over as an unfortunate by-product of the prevailing hostilities.

The king, at any rate, had more important matters on his mind in 1346, and matters in which he was heavily dependent on the services of the likes of Smale and his fellow shipmen, so he had reason to be indulgent. In September, Edward's forces laid siege to Calais. In so doing, they were supported by a fleet of 690 ships, manned by 14,040 mariners assembled from English ports and thirty-eight ships and 805 sailors from abroad. Of these, Dartmouth provided no fewer than thirty-one ships and 757 seamen and, while the part which they played is not specifically reported, the involvement of the town and its luminaries in the French expedition is hinted at elsewhere – in the recorded mobilisation of Guy de Bryan, accompanied by six esquires and six archers. Guy de Bryan was knighted on the 26th of August of that year and it is highly likely that the ceremony took place on the battlefield of Crécy, on the eve of Edward's famous victory there.

While John Hawley, as the precocious small son of a Dartmouth ship-owner, may have been vaguely aware of the *Marie Magdaleine* incident and its aftermath at the time, he was clearly much too young to have been directly involved in it. Talk of this and other similar exploits would, however, have formed much of the background noise of his family and social life as a child and young man. And he was certainly old enough to have had direct experience of a similar incident, also involving Smale, which occurred later and became the subject of litigation in 1361:

On March 20th 1361 William Smale was once more being taken to task in a:

"Commission of oyer and terminer [hear and to enquire] *to Robert de Herle, constable of Dover Castle....whereas many merchants, aliens and denizens, freighted a ship of John Goldbeter, John Salaman of England and Jakemart Flemyng, merchants, worth £500,*

---

* *A merciful release, perhaps, from a marriage to one who earned the soubriquet "Pedro the Cruel". He did, however, become an ally of England, albeit one with a mixed reputation, and Chaucer laments his death in* The Monk's Tale.

whereof Christian Roos of Lescluse was master with goods and merchandise to a value of £20,000, at Nauntes in Brittany, to make their profit in Flanders, a large number of evil-doers in ships of William le Smale of Dertemuth and other ships of war in no small number boarded the ship on its way to Flanders, killed the said master and mariners and others therein to the number of 100 persons and brought the ship to Chichester,… thence to ports along the coast to Devon and Cornwall and there disposed of the residue of the cargo.[43]

So here again we see the Dartmouth men privateering off Brittany in some strength; and again doing so, initially at least, with official sanction. Smale was, in this instance, acting as lieutenant to Guy de Bryan, now appointed the King's Admiral of the West, and had assembled seven ships from Dartmouth and eight from other western ports with the express purpose of taking the fight to the king's enemies. The transmogrification of the Dartmouth men from stalwart servants of the Crown into alleged 'evil-doers' may again have been the result of diplomatic manoeuvrings of which, as they patrolled the bays and estuaries of Brittany, they may well have been quite unaware. The exact date of the fight in question is unknown but it is thought to have taken place at some time in 1360. The Treaty of Brétigny was signed in May 1360 and it appears that, by establishing a truce, it may have transformed the status of this Flemish vessel from a potentially legitimate prize of war into a clearly innocent victim of piracy. The Treaty was not ratified until later in the year and this may have complicated the issue. At any rate, for one reason or another, it seems quite possible that the political and therefore legal position was either questionable or simply not known to those involved until after the event.

A ship owned and freighted by a consortium of merchants of various nationalities, even one whose master was apparently Flemish, would always have been vulnerable to seizure by privateers, whose normal practice was to assume that vessels were carrying enemy goods unless it could be proved otherwise. If the crew put up a fight, the privateers seldom took prisoners. Had they been aware of the truce, Smale's men would clearly have been guilty of piracy, although it is apparent that this had not been the original purpose of the expedition. The sudden truce may have deprived the sponsors of the flotilla of any possible source of revenue to defray their considerable costs, and Smale's men, in full knowledge of it, may simply have felt compelled to carry on regardless. William Smale would have been an old man by 1360 – probably in his sixties[†] – and, while it is quite possible that he directed

---

[*] *The valuation of the ship at just £500, against a cargo value of £20,000, gives an interesting indication of how quickly the capital cost of a ship could be defrayed, even in normally profitable trading.*

[†] *Smale may not have been a native Dartmothian; an entry in the Patent Rolls for March 1327 gives "Protection and safe-conduct for William le Smale, master of 'La Juliana' of Southampton, and the mariners of the said ship, going on the King's business to and from the duchy of Aquitaine". It seems highly likely that this was the same man and, if so, the entry gives a clue to his age and establishes his credentials as a professional seaman. He makes his debut appearance as a Dartmouth burgess in 1336.*

the attack in person, it is perhaps more likely that, having assembled, manned and equipped the ships for this officially sanctioned expedition, he had stayed at home in Dartmouth. This is his last appearance in the historical record and the one which seems to have sealed his reputation among historians as a rapacious pirate. All things considered, and calling Guy de Bryan and others as character witnesses, we might ask the jury of history to consider a more lenient verdict[*].

The cast of possible witnesses regarding Smale's presence or absence on this occasion must include the young John Hawley. As the energetic 20 year-old son, and probably by then a principal, of a local ship-owning family, who was to become renowned not only as the town's leading merchant and burgess but also as a man of action, it is quite likely that Hawley was aboard one of the Dartmouth ships which were among the "...*no small number*" involved in the incident. The fight in which so many died is perhaps the nastiest involving Dartmouth privateers to be recorded but it only appears in the historical record because, for what would have been regarded essentially technical reasons, it became the subject of civil litigation and diplomatic concern. Other similar, if less serious, incidents were recorded and many more, where the action fell within the recognised bounds of privateering, would have gone unrecorded. John Hawley was serving his apprenticeship at this time under the leadership of William Smale and his like and, whether or not he witnessed this particular instance of blood-letting and plunder, it is unlikely that he could, in such times, have grown to maturity as a mariner-merchant and remained altogether innocent of such behaviour. It came with the job.

The peace of the 1360s was to be only partial. Edward, as a way of strengthening his bargaining hand, unofficially encouraged continued predations by the wandering mercenary soldiers who remained in France, and the two realms continued to fight a war by proxy in Castile. The French in 1365 intervened in the civil war there, on the side of Henry of Trastamára against his brother, Pedro the Cruel. Edward, the Black Prince, who was always more interested in Spanish dynastic affairs than in those of France, in turn invaded Castile in 1367 in support of Pedro, apparently settling the matter by defeating Henry at the battle of Nájera. What was at stake for France and England in this conflict was control of the Castilian fleet; and the eventual defeat and death of Pedro in 1369, after Edward's withdrawal, was later to have grave consequences for English mariners and for the security of the western and Channel ports.

It is a testament to the resilience of medieval traders that, in a partial peace, and between the visitations of the plague in 1361-2 and 1368-9, trade across the sea managed to recover, albeit in a changed form. The wine trade re-opened and, whilst

---

[*] *He generally seems to have been in good standing with the Crown in 1360, when, in addition to de Bryan's commission, he was entrusted with the inspection of the cargo of an English ship, arrested at sea when bound for Flanders, which was suspected of having been loaded without customs dues being paid.*

exports of raw wool fluctuated wildly around a downward trend, exports of woollen cloth began to see a growth which became sustained in later years. A record for May 1st 1364 gives a clue as to the nature of the local trade at the time:

> "Licence for one year for John Clerc of Dartmouth, merchant, to ship in the port of that town and take to Gascony and Spain forty fardels [bundles] of strait cloths called 'backes' bought in the county of Devon to trade with there and to buy and to bring from those ports to England wine, salt and iron."[44]

The Dartmouth shipmen seem, on the whole, to have reverted to less contentious activities during this period, and this gave Hawley the opportunity to develop the more peaceable aspects of his profession. The naval and commercial rolls do record some allegations of misappropriation of ships and their cargoes during this interlude but such complaints seem to have been the result of commercial disputes or simple thievery and no longer arose from the vagaries of privateering in a shifting political milieu.

Politics, however, continued to influence the activities of seamen and the fact that most maritime activities at this time had to be licensed, and the closely prescriptive nature of the licences granted, reflects the continuing diplomatic tensions and the ever-present potential for renewed hostilities. The licences also provide an insight into the nature of the trade in logistical support to the military, which in the 1360s was quite a significant business for Dartmouth. In particular, the port played its part in serving the requirements of the Black Prince in his continental expeditions. In January 1368, for example, licence was granted to Walter Penhirgard, 'chivaler', to take ship from Dartmouth to Aquitaine with an esquire, 6 archers, 24 horses, 10 grooms, £8 for his expenses and a letter of exchange for £20[45]. Elsewhere, among the hundreds of similar entries in the Patent Rolls at that time, we see the minute detail of the licensing system extending down, in the case of one yeoman's 1367 excursion to Brittany, to:

> "...8 bows, 2 dozen arrows and 10 marks [£6 13s 4d] for his expenses."[46]

The resumption of hostilities in 1369 brought about an immediate collapse of normal trade, as the wine growers of Gascony fled Charles' advancing troops and the grapes withered on the vines. The need to ship soldiers and *materiel*, however, became acute and, although the profits to be had from logistical shipping can be assumed to have been less attractive than those of shipping and principal trading in wool and wine, the sums involved were not insignificant. Ship's masters were typically earning a comparatively generous, and seemingly inflation-adjusted, rate of sixpence per day and their crewmen threepence per day "...by reason of the dearness of provisions that year..." and the record for payments made at Dartmouth in May-July 1370 to masters and seamen in respect of their carrying officers and soldiers to Gascony, which totalled £1,266 13s. 4d, bespeaks a lively enough trade.[47]

In military terms, the English were, by the time of Hawley's first appearance as owner of *Le James* in 1372, firmly on the back foot. The once-vigorous Edward III was ageing and the Black Prince had retreated to England in 1371, his reputation in tatters after the brutal sacking of Limoges, and suffering from a gastro-intestinal disease which was soon to kill him. Gascony had fallen into protracted and ruinous warfare and the French had been able to re-take most of the lands ceded in 1360. Things were no better at sea as, in June 1372, the fleet of the earl of Pembroke was attacked and destroyed off La Rochelle by the galleys of Charles' Castilian allies.

The realm of Edward III thus faced greater and more widespread threats in the September of 1372 than it had in the years following the victories of Sluys, Crécy and Poitiers. Ever the soldier, Edward characteristically determined to go on the offensive and Wauter Haulegh's seizure of the Dartmouth ships for the king's service and the instruction to the masters of the ships to assemble at Southampton would have been intended to augment the forces for what had originally been conceived as a continental campaign. This had, of necessity, turned into an expedition to relieve La Rochelle, which had earlier in the year come under blockade by another Castilian squadron, which had joined forces with a French force. In the event, adverse winds prevented even this intervention, which was abandoned in October, by which time it was known that La Rochelle had anyway surrendered in August[*]. Thus, if Hawley's *James* and the other arrested Dartmouth ships went anywhere in the autumn of 1372, it was to no avail.

The John Hawley of September 1372 was, at the age of thirty-two or so, a wealthy, well established and influential figure in a small but disproportionately important port. His father's business, painstakingly built on land reclaimed from the mud adjoining the fosse in the early years of the war, had been developed in a community whose enterprise extended beyond conventional trade into military logistics and privateering. This was the man who, at some time in the latter part of 1373, almost certainly met Geoffrey Chaucer.

In the autumn of 1372, just as Hawley was being instructed to send the *James* into the king's service at Southampton, Chaucer, who is thought to have been Hawley's age, or perhaps a year or two younger, was serving as an esquire in Edward III's chamber and was sent as a junior member of a trading mission to Genoa, there to negotiate the designation of a particular English seaport for the use of Genoese merchants. It seems likely that Chaucer was selected for this duty because he had acquired some knowledge of Italian, as a result of his childhood acquaintance with the Italian merchants with whom his vintner father did business. The specific outcome of this six-month journey, which also took in Florence, is not known, but Genoese ships did thereafter make much more extensive use of Southampton than they had previously.

---

[*] *The English garrison is said to have surrendered as a result of its illiterate commander being duped by the town's mayor in a cleverly-crafted ruse de guerre involving what he claimed to be a letter from Edward III.*

The unruly Dartmothians, however, threw a spanner in the diplomatic works when, in 1373, the local mayor and bailiff arrested a cargo vessel, the *Saint Mary and Saint George*, described as a 'tarita" belonging to Johan de Nigris of Genoa.[48] For what reason, or on what pretext the ship was seized is unknown† but Percy Russell suggests that she was probably a large, blue-water trading vessel which the Westcountry cogs could not have taken on in a sea fight. If, however, she was obliged by weather conditions or by having suffered some damage to seek refuge in the nearest port, in this case Dartmouth, she would have been at the mercy of her hosts. She may just have been too tempting a prize.

The timing of this incident was clearly embarrassing to Edward, who sent Chaucer – the obvious choice perhaps, given his recent dealings with the Genoese – to Dartmouth to sort it out. There are two conflicting dates for this commission: August 20th and November 11th 1373. Whichever the date of his visit, the young Geoffrey carried with him heavyweight royal authority; all sheriffs, mayors, bailiffs and others were ordered to render him assistance. The local worthies, therefore, would have been both obliged and, in the circumstances, keen to turn out in force to meet him. There is an unusual gap in the mayoral records and it is not clear who was mayor in 1373, but the next man recorded in the office is John Hawley himself. He was elected mayor on September 29th 1374. As for the likely supporting cast of local luminaries who would have presented themselves to the king's envoy, it is easy enough to guess. The roll call of officials and signatories who regularly featured in the various records throughout the century naturally changed over time, but it has a high degree of consistency over any shorter period. The same names keep cropping up as parties to recorded events and transactions or as witnesses thereto and, as with the three John Hawleys, we can see members of several of the prominent families of the town appearing across two or more generations.

We can imagine the mayor and burgesses who met Chaucer, eager to demonstrate their respectability, loyalty to the Crown and generally God-fearing nature, putting on a good show; perhaps showing off their latest symbol of civic pride – the newly consecrated Trinity Church. In this and in the wining and dining which no doubt took the edge off of the recriminations and hard negotiations, Chaucer almost certainly met most or all of the following:

"John Haulegh, Benedict Bottesana, John Clerc, William Knoll, William Clerc, Richard Gordon, John Knoll, Thomas Renald, William Hikke, John Asshenden, John Briton, Richard Henry and Thomas de Asshenden."[49]

---

* *A general description of any ship which could carry cargo and was not designed exclusively for warfare. Genoese ships of the time were notably advanced in their design.*

† *A manufactured dispute over customs duty is one of the more likely possibilities.*

This list offers itself because it was these men who were commissioned by the king in 1374 and again (with the omission of *William Hikke*) in 1377, to ensure that the defences of the town were in a fit state "...*in consideration of the damage and reproach which might befall the town of Dertemuth...*" Such was the nature of this commission that we must assume that this was a list of Dartmouth's most senior and trusted commoners.

It is also noteworthy that, of these thirteen, six are known to have been shipowners and at least two others to have been involved in maritime trade. Among these, John Hawley, Thomas Asshenden, Benedict de Bottesana and William and John Knoll appear most frequently over the years in positions of power and influence. By this time, the shipowners really were running the town and we do not need to draw on the evidence of their subsequent collaborative ventures to see them as a close-knit group, bound by personal friendships.

It is no wonder, then, that Chaucer, as a keen and humorous observer of contemporary society, when surrounded by this doubtless affable crew, all intent on fending off a potentially serious charge of piracy and restoring themselves to the royal favour, was provided with a rich store of raw material for his subsequent portrait of the Shipman. And, even among this group, which epitomised the merchant warrior class of the time, it is likely that Hawley, an obviously able and energetic man of about Chaucer's own age, would have stood out.

Hawley was soon to take on civic office and become Dartmouth's foremost spokesman for an extended period during which the town, the region and the realm came under constant threat from beyond the sea and when the control exercised by the sovereign was dangerously weak. The times were to call for a combination of responsible civic leadership and energetic opportunism and, while Chaucer's wry description of the Shipman highlighted more of the latter than the former, it was Hawley's embodiment of both these qualities which gave rise to his subsequent fame and notoriety.

The Privateer Mayor: 1377-1388

By the summer of 1377 John Hawley was serving his second term as mayor and had become, by some distance, Dartmouth's wealthiest and most powerful man. He and his wife, Joan, were living in a substantial residence with four domestic servants.* He employed a significant portion of the town's population of 679 adults and owned no fewer than forty-five of their houses, in addition to his wharves and ships. However, if John and Joan Hawley were living in considerable comfort, the poll tax records for that year suggest that the opulence of their household was

---

* *There is some doubt as to whether he was already living in the house in Clifton which was eventually to become the Guildhall or, as the poll tax record seems to imply, somewhere on the other side of the fosse in Hardness.*

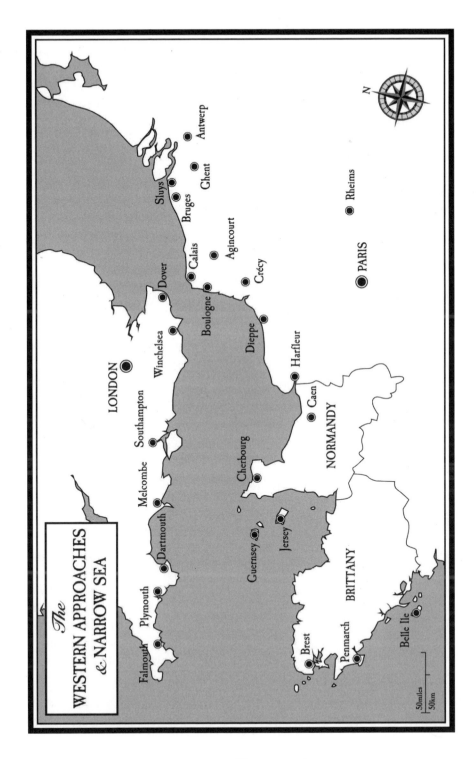

The
WESTERN APPROACHES
& NARROW SEA

Falmouth
Plymouth
Dartmouth
Melcombe
Southampton
LONDON
Winchelsea
Dover
Calais
Sluys
Bruges
Ghent
Antwerp
Boulogne
Dieppe
Harfleur
Crécy
Agincourt
PARIS
Rheims
Caen
NORMANDY
Cherbourg
Guernsey
Jersey
BRITTANY
Brest
Penmarch
Belle Ile

N

50 miles
50 km

exceeded by that of Thomas and Joan Asshenden*. Asshenden's household, the largest in Dartmouth, included his widowed mother, Avice, and had no fewer than six servants. The family was, in 1387, granted permission to have mass said in their own oratory, suggesting that they lived in considerable style.[50]

Thomas Asshenden was probably ten years or so Hawley's senior but they clearly had a close relationship and their lives were variously intertwined until Asshenden's death in 1393. The activities of the Asshenden family in several ways foreshadowed those of the Hawleys and it is very likely that Thomas became, if not a conscious role model, at least a close friend of Hawley and one whose example had a considerable influence on him. The possibility that Thomas's father, William, had been a substitute paternal role model for the young John has already been suggested. In all, the relationship between the families probably extended across three generations. Thomas preceded Hawley in obtaining royal letters patent, exempting him from holding office under the Crown against his will for a period of twenty years from 1372. He nonetheless acted as deputy butler in all the ports of Devon and held various other prestigious public appointments, while continuing in trading and other maritime activities. Thomas is not known to have held the office of mayor, although he must be one of the most likely candidates to fill the gaps in the records for 1370 and/or 1373. His career, like Hawley's, combined private enterprise with public service; like Hawley, he served as a Member of Parliament for Dartmouth four times. While he perhaps did not have quite Hawley's capacity for aggressive opportunism, some incidents in his life suggest that, in this regard also, they were from the same mould. The two were later to embark on collaborative privateering enterprises and travelled to Westminster together to represent Dartmouth in the Parliament of 1390.

Asshenden was a prosperous second-generation shipowner but, by 1377, it was the career of Hawley that was manifestly in the ascendant. Anyone doing business with Dartmouth at that time would soon find themselves dealing with the second John Hawley, as merchant, landlord, shipowner or mayor.

The events of that summer, however, were soon to put an end to any prospects he, Asshenden or any of their fellow burgesses may have had of a routinely affluent life. On June 21st Edward III died. His eldest son, Edward, the Black Prince, would have succeeded him but had died the previous year, probably of stomach cancer, at the age of forty. The crown therefore passed to Edward III's ten-year-old grandson, Richard, who was to reign as Richard II. His accession, under an uneasy collective regency, led by his uncle, John of Gaunt, marked the beginning of a period of instability and insecurity in English politics which was to form the backdrop to Hawley's activities for the next two decades and more.

---

* The poll tax of 1377 was levied at a rate of 4d. for each member of the household but, by specifying servants as such, gives an indication of the comparative affluence of some residents.

And trouble was not long in coming. With Edward's death, a two-year truce with France came to an end and just three days later, on June 24th, a formidable, combined squadron of fifty French, Castilian, Genoese and Portuguese vessels and four thousand men, under the French admiral, Jean de Vienne[*] embarked on a cruise during which they attacked a number of southern and western towns, including Dartmouth. The Castilian galleys, in particular, posed a threat to which the English had no ready response; whilst Edward had possessed a royal squadron of forty or so ships early in his reign, this had dwindled to no more than five when he died. Under the young Richard, the Crown owned no ships at all and thus, more than ever, the safeguard of the seas was to fall to the merchant shipmen.

The young Richard II, the weakness of whose rule created the chaos in which Hawley thrived.
Portrait dated c.1390 at Westminster Abbey

It is tempting to imagine Hawley at this point, as a resourceful local leader in the prime of his life, putting to sea, as master of one of his own ships, to direct the defence of the surrounding sea. The more probable, if disappointingly prosaic, truth is that in the late 1370s he was simply too busy to do anything of the kind. He was, for example, in June 1378, among four Westcountry officials commissioned to police the movements of vessels which had been arrested for the king's service but had failed to appear; and it was not until he handed over the mayoralty to Richard Harry in 1379 that he was able sufficiently to free himself of such official encumbrances as to engage in privateering on his own account.

With the resumption of hostilities, the more or less routine plundering by Dartmouth mariners of any ship which might, under any pretext, be deemed to be in the service of the enemy had also resumed. John and Hugh Weston of Dartmouth were in January 1378 called to Westminster to answer charges that they had, in an Exeter ship together with a Dartmouth vessel,...

> "...set upon Stephen de la Fawrie and his fellows of Bayonne, claimed a share of a ship of Bilbawe in Spain, laden with wines, which his vessel, when on the king's service and at the king's charges, with one of Dertemuth, had captured at Tristram in Britanny..."[51]

After various disputes and struggles with the plaintiff's crew, the Westons were alleged to have forced them to sail the ship, together with its cargo of wine, to

---

[*] *Jean de Vienne was a career soldier and administrator who had been governor of Calais when it surrendered to Edward III's forces. He was appointed Admiral of France in 1373, a role in which he was highly effective.*

Dartmouth, where they detained it. It is clear that, in this case, the plaintiff was not the merchant of Bilbao, whose ship was presumably carrying a French cargo and was therefore fair game, but a rival privateer out of Bayonne. How the case turned out is not known but suffice it to say that the Westons appear to have overcome what, if any, difficulty this summons may have caused them and Hugh, at any rate, appears repeatedly as an active and apparently prosperous privateer several years later. Nor did it prevent the brothers from subsequently being appointed to a borough office; Hugh was bailiff of Dartmouth in 1391 and was succeeded in that role by John in 1392.

Predictably, Hawley, once freed from his mayoral duties, joined with his associates to put together a more substantial enterprise. On December 1st 1379, licence was granted to Hawley, Asshenden and Benedict de Bottesana *"to go to sea at their own charges under the King's protection for one year from the feast of the Purification* [early February] *to attack and destroy his enemies..."*[52] There was no need, at this time, for Hawley or the other burgesses to obtain a licence to undertake privateering as such. Rather, the value of the licence lay in the limited protection which it offered against arrest for less lucrative service to the king. Of the seven vessels named in the licence, three were described as barges owned by John Hawley (*"la Mighel"*, *"la Joutte"* and *"la Cog Johan"*). Asshenden's *"la Seintsavourscogg"* is also described as a barge and de Bottesana's *"la Alisote"* as a balinger. This suggests that the owners regarded at least two of the barges to be small cogs. The remaining two vessels, described as 'ships' were presumably larger cogs. The owners of these were not specified (being described simply as *"of Dertemuth"*) and it is probable that they were jointly owned. One of these was called *"la Katerine"*; the other, tantalisingly to Chaucer scholars, bore the name: *"la Magdelayne"*.

It is not known whether the vessels thus licensed ever embarked on their intended expedition, nor whether their principals went to sea in person. There is no record, in the admiralty courts, of any proceedings relating to the period, in which any of them were cited and both Hawley and Asshenden are named as witnesses to property conveyances on June 7th and September 27th 1380, putting them firmly ashore for the four months in the middle of the term of the licence. It is, of course, not impossible that one, two or all three of them went to sea for some period in the spring or winter of 1380, but neither is there any positive evidence that they or anyone else actually did so. The odds are that Hawley was, at most, a vicarious privateer at this time.

The only record which incontrovertibly places Hawley and Asshenden at sea refers to the early months of 1384 and it does not portray aggressive privateering. Charles V had died in 1380 and the removal of a bellicose monarch on one side of the conflict afforded scope for the pacifist, seventeen year-old king on the other to be more assertive in his overtures for peace. At the end of 1383, Richard commissioned his uncles, John of Gaunt and the duke of Buckingham, to negotiate a truce, which was subsequently extended to the winter of 1384. It was during this truce, and having taken the additional precaution of obtaining a letter of safe conduct from the duke of Brittany, that Hawley and Asshenden, with four other Dartmouth merchants, set sail in *La Marie* and *La Trinite* for Brittany with a cargo valued at £300. The truce and the letter of safe conduct, however, turned out to be of very limited value in that, upon their arrival, the Dartmouth ships were forcibly boarded by a number of Bretons who tore up the safe conduct and threw the pieces over the side, assaulted Hawley and the other merchants and their crew and extracted ransom.[53]

The Bretons may have been acting in retaliation for some earlier action by Dartmouth men and Hawley duly sued for recompense in the court of the duke of Brittany and elsewhere to no apparent effect, before petitioning the king, who ordered John de Roches, Admiral of the South and West, to arrest the accused Bretons if he found them within his jurisdiction. There is no record of his bringing the perpetrators to book[*] and it is possible that indignation at this treatment, at a time when he was ostensibly protected by both royal and ducal authority in France, and the failure of Roches to do him justice, brought about a change in John Hawley's attitude to privateering. He certainly appears in a much more combative light – with palpable bad blood between him and Roches – in a subsequent, celebrated case which has been the subject of some substantial academic research.

The events surrounding what was to become known as the '*Batel of Hawley's Barge*' were the subject of legal proceedings, first in Brest in 1388 and then in the Court of Chivalry, before the Constable and Marshal of England, from 1393-1401. [54]

The evidence in the case of *John de Roches v. John Hawley* gives highly detailed but largely contradictory accounts of the events of March 1386. It is, in part, the same story told from different points of view, but it is also in part a near-verbatim record of blatant perjury on one part or the other or, more likely, both. Whatever version of events we may choose to believe, it provides a fascinating insight into the thinking and behaviour of fourteenth-century men of various ranks in a complex situation. The story, as variously told, is broadly as follows:

On the morning of March 2nd 1386, five small French trading vessels, described as 'crayers', laden with wine and other stores, were lying close inshore in the Bay of Audierne, some thirty miles south of Brest, on the southern side of Cap Sizun. At least two were grounded on the sand, while the other three may have been warped out into the deeper water of the inlet.

That morning, the '*barge of Mortrigo*', owned by John Hawley and skippered by John Piers of Hardness and three other vessels – a balinger owned and commanded by Peter Risshenden of Dartmouth, and a barge out of Calais and another of Cherbourg, were sailing southwards from the waters off Pointe St Mathieu, to the West of Brest, where, with others, they had been lying in wait for enemy vessels from which they intended 'to make their profit'. Risshenden's balinger, being faster

---

[*] *It appears that at least La Trinite, which was jointly owned by Hawley and Asshenden, may have been recovered, as she herself captured a Flemish vessel in 1386. This was, however, a common name for ships at the time and they may have given it to another vessel.*

than her consorts, was the first to arrive off Audierne and aboard her was one Richard Scoce, a young cousin of John Hawley[*]. His eye-witness testimony was central to what was presented in court as Hawley's version of events.

According to Scoce, three of the crayers were bound together at anchor, in preparation for combat, as the balinger approached and, when Risshenden hailed them and demanded to know where they were from, they replied that they were from Morlaix and St Gildas in Brittany and immediately attacked the balinger with a variety of projectile weapons: two guns, quarrels and darts. As the balinger came alongside, they fought hand to hand with glaives[†], lances and hatchets. In the mêlée, Risshenden was wounded in the leg by a stone, a man called Patrike in the leg, and one Benet in the arm while John Cornyssh received a stomach wound from a *virriton*[‡] of which he died four days later. Risshenden broke off the fight and the Cherbourg balinger, which had by this time arrived on the scene, was in turn repulsed. It was only when the larger, slower, barges came in sight that the Bretons decided that discretion was the better part of valour and took to their boats to flee to the nearby shore. At midday, the Englishmen duly took possession of the crayers and their cargoes, as legitimate prizes of war. The following evening, the prize crews started north to St Mathieu, where the spoils were divided – the largest crayer, of fifty-five tuns, being awarded to the Calais and Cherbourg vessels, that of thirty tuns to Hawley's barge and the smallest, of fifteen tuns, to Risshenden's balinger.

The master of one of the captured crayers, Robert Kermerwar, gave an entirely different account of events. In his version, Hawley's men had arrived the previous day and had approached the crayers by land, when all five were beached. They were told, he says, that the five ships had been given safe passage to Brest by Sir John de Roches, captain of that port, for the purpose of victualling the castle and town and that Roches had posted one guard on each ship. This testimony was corroborated by Yon Stopard, the part-owner and master of one of the other crayers, the *Saint Pierre de Plumauger*, who added, interestingly, that one half of the victuals in the crayers had been ordered for stocking the castle and town of Brest.

The Breton version of events was elaborated by John Doway, who stated, when asked if the crayers had been taken by Hawley on the high seas, that the three crayers were captured whilst still beached by the four ships, led by the 'black barge" of Dartmouth and that their crews had "...*not two swords among them, apart from those which the guards had.*" Although the testimony of these and other witnesses for Roches is sometimes apparently inconsistent with regard to some points, they were

---

[*] *When making his sworn deposition, he says that he is: "Richard Scoce, of free birth, literate, of thirty years or about, of the county of Devonshire..." and that "...he has known John Hawley for about twenty years and confesses that he is a cousin of John Hawley" (White, op.cit. p.379)*

[†] *A single-edged pole weapon, similar to a pike*

[‡] *A bow that shot a whirling dart*

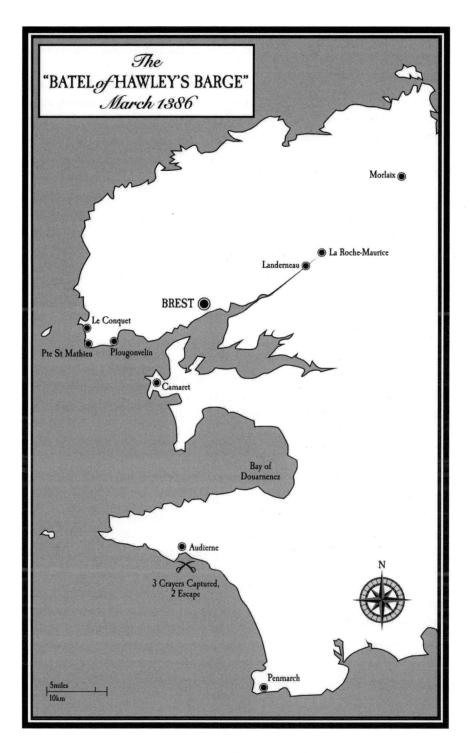

The
"BATEL of HAWLEY'S BARGE"
March 1386

Morlaix

La Roche-Maurice
Landerneau

BREST

Le Conquet

Pte St Mathieu   Plougonvelin

Camaret

Bay of
Douarnenez

Audierne

3 Crayers Captured,
2 Escape

N

Penmarch

5miles
10km

all agreed that Hawley's men were fully aware that the ships had been given safe passage to Brest, one going as far as to say that it had been read to them and that they had *"said that it was good and sufficient"*.

To the extent that they were able to find disinterested witnesses in the situation in which they found themselves, Hawley's men do seem to have been at pains to prepare evidence for their story, which they obviously expected to be challenged, by showing their various wounds to Nicholas Gybbes, a Dartmouth mariner who was in Brest at the time, and by inviting him to the burial of John Cornyssh. While this throws into doubt the Breton testimony that, unarmed and essentially defenceless, they had fled without a fight, their contention that safe passage had been granted to them was not actually disputed. The question in that regard was as to when it had been issued and whether it had been shown to Hawley's men before the initial engagement.

It was subsequently stated, on Hawley's behalf, that Philip Derneforde, lieutenant to Roches, knowing of the presence of the privateers in the area and conscious of the threat which they posed to the crayers at Audierne, had invited some of the ships' masters to dine with him in Brest and, whilst they were thus occupied, had the safe conduct documents drawn up and conveyed overland to the masters of the crayers, in order that they might arrive before the privateers did. The five soldiers sent as guards certainly testified that they had carried the documents with them but the timing remains in doubt.

What was not in doubt, however, was that three of the five ships and their cargoes had been spirited away by Hawley's associates, and their owners consequently filed suit against Roches *ex officio* for restitution. They had more luck than Hawley had with regard to his similar experience of 1384 and, in August 1388, in the Constable's Court in Brest, Roches was fined eight thousand francs and ordered additionally to recompense the owners of the crayers and cargo for his failure to enforce the safe passage.[*]

This was doubtless annoying for Roches, who had been in England while the events in question had occurred but, if that had been all there was to it, his subsequent action against Hawley for recompense in relation to the fine and compensation awarded against him would have been straightforward enough. It is interesting that Hawley alone was cited as the respondent, although he had been a minor beneficiary of the action[†], suggesting that nobody was in any doubt as to who was the *de facto* admiral of this particular privateering group. This was in spite of the fact that, throughout the whole affair, he had been at home in Dartmouth, once again discharging his mayoral duties.

The allegations in the pleadings of the plaintiff are plain enough; they also belie the complexity of what was to become a somewhat bizarre trial:

---

[*] *It is ironic that, for just under two years, from May 1386, the Constable of Brest was none other than Thomas Asshenden and, although he appears to have moved on before the judgement was made, he may have had some influence over the proceedings. If so, this may have influenced Roches' attitude to Dartmothians in general.*

[†] *Hawley's half share amounted to fifteen tuns of wine.*

Foss Street, Dartmouth: The mill dam and conduit that linked Clifton-Dartmouth with Hardness. Hawley's Hoe was reclaimed land to the left of the foreground.
Courtesy of Nigel Evans

St Saviour's Church – consecrated as the Trinity Church in 1372.

Courtesy of Dave Cawley Dartmouth.TV www.dartmouth.tv

The Dartmouth Museum's model of Hawley's Christopher *– ships of the time sometimes had elaborately decorated sails.*
Courtesy of Dartmouth Museum

Hawley's arms.
– Hawley was elevated to armigerous rank by Richard II on May 16th 1395. The horns are thought by some to represent the trumpets with which his seamen were summoned but are perhaps more likely a nod in the direction of Dartmouth's feudal lord, Guy de Bryan, whose crest features a similar device.
Courtesy of Dartmouth Museum

The Arms of Dartmouth echo the circumstances of the Borough's origins.
Courtesy of Dartmouth Museum

Blackpool Sands, as viewed from the direction of du Châtel's advance –
The defending militia was arrayed on the far slope.
Courtesy of Valerie Wills

Previous double page spread: "venerabilis vir" – *The memorial brass*
of John Hawley and his wives – Joan and Alice.
Courtesy of Norsworthy Photography

Dartmouth Castle: The gun fort was developed later on the site of Hawley's fortalice, the remains of whose curtain wall can be seen to the left rear of the picture.
Courtesy of Kevin Pyne

John Hawley's house in Higher Street, Dartmouth (second left) which was the Guildhall from 1494 to 1864.

From a painting by Miss E.Hunt, 1839

A trail (right) of the Hawley plaques and signs that can still be seen all over Dartmouth (in descending order):
1. Dartmouth & Kingswear Society Millennium plaque in Newcomen Road marking the approximate site of Hawley's house (see above).
2. Street sign in Hauley Road that runs from Fairfax Place to the North Embankment.
3. Hawley's coat of arms displayed (left) on the Gallery of St.Saviour's Church, (right) above 29, Fairfax Place (and another see page 83 in Dartmouth Museum in the Butterwalk).
4. Doorway to the Freemason's Hauley Lodge No.797 at Hauley Hall off Lower Street.
5. English Heritage plaque on the remaining curtain wall of Hawley's fortalice at Dartmouth Castle.
6. Hauley VI, the latest Lower Ferry tug to bear the name Hauley since the first in 1909.

"...There came certain men of John Hawley, the second day of March in the ninth year of our lord King Richard, by authority of the said John Hawley, and attacked and took the said vessels with the victuals from the possession of the lieges and guards of our lord the King, notwithstanding the aforesaid safe conduct, and overcoming them in the haven of Ponte-croys* and within the raunsons† of our said lord the King at Brest. And they sent them away to the said John Hawley, and the said John Hawley approved and sanctioned the said robbery and made distribution of the spoils. Thus he notoriously and feloniously sanctioned and confirmed the said crime..."

Taking this at face value, the only point at issue would have been whether or not the safe custody order had been delivered before Risshenden hove alongside the feisty crayers, or, taking the Breton version of the facts, Hawley's ruffians had fallen on the righteous and defenceless merchantmen, in Audierne Bay. The events of the days which followed the capture of the crayers and the various ways in which these events were represented were, however, to make the whole affair much more complicated.

The complication surrounds what happened next to the other two ships which Hawley's men encountered at Audierne. Whether they had remained beached or whether Philip Derneforde's soldiers had managed to get them away before the privateers arrived, they had somehow managed to escape capture. Derneforde had meanwhile been informed, presumably by messenger travelling overland, of what had happened and approached Perkyn Dobyn, master of Hawley's 'big barge' *Trinity*, one of two of Hawley's vessels which were making ready for sea in Brest harbour, and Michael Kykard master of one of three barges belonging to Hugh Weston which were also there, and asked them in which direction they intended to sail. Dobyn and Kykard replied "Toward the south". Realising that they would therefore almost certainly meet the two remaining ships which were making their way north from Audierne by a predictable route across the outer part of the Bay of Douarnenez, Derneforde then made a verbal statement of their safe passage, saying:

"You will meet two vessels with topcastles, belonging to Guyhomar Maufuric, loaded with wine from Rochelle, which wine we have bought for victualling the castle and city of Brest; for this reason, we ask that you allow the said two vessels to come freely to us."

As expected, the Dartmouth men did meet the two ships and a witness for Hawley tells that, after interrogating Derneforde's men, Perkyn Dobyn had let them sail on to Brest, having made the caveat that, if their story turned out to be false, he would seek restitution. The witness to this conversation says nothing of Dobyn having placed some of his own men on board the ships in order to ensure

---

* *Pont-Croix – three miles upstream from Audierne.*

† *Ransom, signifying domain.*

fair play but Nicholas Gybbes' subsequent testimony implies that he must have done. At any rate, Dobyn and the others, a few days later, were forced by adverse weather to return to Brest, where they again encountered the two ships, which had still not unloaded their cargoes. Seeing the approach of the privateers, the two ships hastily made sail and headed north-eastwards, up the estuary of the Elorn, to unload at Landerneau, which, being outside the jurisdiction of Brest, was, except at times of truce, an enemy port. It was in relation to this movement that, years later, accusations were to fly and tempers to become frayed.

Gybbes, testifying on behalf of Hawley, stated that he had been present in Brest when the two vessels with topcastles came into the harbour and that he estimated that one had a capacity of seventy tuns of wine and the other of more than sixty tuns. He said that some of Hawley's men were aboard, to guard the ships, during their three- or four-day stay but that they had been driven out by Bretons and by 'certain men of Sir John de Roches', who ordered the ships to Landerneau. Hawley's side also alleged that Derneforde had confessed to receiving a bribe of two tuns of wine from each of the vessels and one franc for each tun they carried. The implication was clear enough but Hawley went further, accusing Roches of facilitating the provisioning of the enemy camp of 'Roche Morys' near Landerneau, in exchange for bribes – a clear act of treason.

Hawley laid this accusation of treason before the Court of Chivalry on October 24th 1393 and a copy was delivered to Roches on the following day. Roches' reaction was an explosion of chivalric indignation. He immediately demanded that he be allowed to settle the matter by personal combat with Hawley and threw down his gauntlet in the court, one of a number of occasions on which he made such demands.

The legal technicalities of this case, involving issues such as jurisdiction and admissibility of evidence, may be of interest to legal historians but what is striking to the lay observer is the extent to which men who were undoubtedly religious and in fear of royal authority were prepared, having sworn on stacks of bibles in the presence of persons of great importance and authority, to perjure themselves. And perjure themselves they surely did, causing a significant part of the trial proceedings to consist of witnesses asserting their honesty and independence, while their opponents impugned their character and motives. It is clear that even someone of Roches' eminence was not averse to representing the facts in whatever way met his immediate purpose, and changing his mind later when it suited him. In the trial at Brest in 1388, he asserted that "...*the ships which Hawley took were not in the haven of Pontecroys but on the high sea.*" If true, this would have absolved him of responsibility for restitution to the merchants, but it is clear that the Constable's Court was not convinced, otherwise they would have immediately ceded jurisdiction to an admiralty court, which they did not. He subsequently, and perhaps understandably, made the opposite claim in the Court of Chivalry.

Both sides produced scores of witnesses, many of whom made sworn statements, under a commission to John Corp, in the Trinity church in Dartmouth or in various locations in Brest, and most of whom seem to have been of dubious independence. Roches made a particular show of trying to discredit Hawley's witnesses, most of whom he rightly accused of either having benefited from the seizure of the ships or otherwise to be in Hawley's employ. He also took particular exception to the testimony of two witnesses, who, according to him "...*quite evidently perjured themselves for they say that the two ships with topcastles were taken to Roche Morys, which is impossible since Roche Morys is a great distance from the sea*". In this latter point he is guilty of either misrepresentation or pedantry; La Roche Maurice was then, and still is, about four miles from the water's edge in Landerneau – no great distance for the carts and pack animals which would in any case have been used once the cargo was unloaded. Roches also somewhat undermined his own show of confidence by stating that *if* the wine had been shipped to Landerneau, it had happened during a truce between Brest and Roche Maurice, while he was in England, suggesting that he had a somewhat tenuous grasp of the facts.

Hawley's riposte to Roches' denigration of his witnesses was hardly more creditable; he asserted that many of Roches' witnesses were not competent, their having been excommunicated as schismatics. In all, it is clear that, as in most medieval trials of this kind, it was not the intention of either party to achieve a just settlement but rather to win.

Roches and Hawley never met in mortal combat; the case dragged on for seven years and, after Roches' death in 1399, it came to an inconclusive end in October 1401, over fifteen years after the events to which it pertained. Assessing who, if anyone, was in the right in a six-hundred-year-old courtroom drama, in which it is clear that many of the witnesses were lying, is an interesting, if ultimately fruitless, diversion. Roches' two most credible witnesses with regard to what happened at Audierne – the crayers' masters – by this time had nothing material to gain from supporting Roches, but some of their testimony appears to have been at odds with some incontrovertible facts and they may have been motivated by simple dislike of the Dartmothians. Richard Scoce's testimony holds together well and has a ring of truth about it – whilst also having the corpse of the unfortunate John Cornyssh, interred at the abbey above the cliffs of St Mathieu, to support his version of events. The bad-tempered nature of the proceedings appears to have been in marked contrast to the generally matter-of-fact, pragmatic adjudications in other cases involving privateers. The sums involved in the case were comparatively modest and Hawley's allegation of treason as part of his countersuit seems rather extreme and certainly provocative.

One scholar suggests an intriguing possible explanation for the heat that this incident generated. In a separate case in August 1387, Hawley and Roches were under joint sentence of restitution in respect of theft of twenty-one tuns of wine by men of Dartmouth under Hawley and Bretons under Roches. Perhaps the animosity between the two men resulted from a falling-out over the division of the spoils of their joint privateering activity[55]. If so, perhaps, behind his indignant bluster, the King's Admiral of the West and captain of Brest was a deeply corrupt man. This seems unlikely. Roches had only been appointed to the captaincy of Brest a few weeks before the incident and had a respectable record of diligent and efficient preparation of the port and castle against attack and siege – an eventuality which actually arose in the early summer of that year, the French forces being beaten off with the assistance of John of Gaunt, whose troops were passing en route to Castile.

A more likely cause of Roche's exasperation was that, when he was subsequently dismissed as captain of Brest by the Lords Appellant in 1388, to be replaced by the earl of Arundel, he was held liable for debts and damages incurred on behalf of the garrison during his tenure. Arundel went as far as to sue Roches for over £5,000 and, on his refusal to appear in court to answer charges, he was declared outlaw[56]. He retained the confidence of the king, however and, when Richard regained the initiative, he was rehabilitated, being briefly appointed Admiral for the North and West in 1389, although it was not until May 1392 that the outlawry was formally pardoned. Hawley may have been acting cynically by accusing Roches of treason in 1393, the claim being nothing more than an attempt to muddy the waters. However, while it is perhaps dangerous to read much into the exact wording of a six hundred year-old testimony translated from a foreign language and possibly taken out of context, Yon Stopard's statement that half of the victuals aboard at least the *Saint Pierre de Plumauger* were for the supply of Brest raises the question as to where the other half was bound. Any other destination – and it seems that the destination was Landerneau or possibly Roche Maurice – would have been enemy territory and Hawley may, technically at least, have had a point.

The whole puzzle might be resolved if there were any evidence that Derneforde, with or without Roches' knowledge, had made a pragmatic deal with the crayer skippers to receive the supplies he urgently needed in return for *de facto* safe conduct for the remainder of their cargos to Landerneau and they had sweetened the deal for him with a quantity of wine and some cash. This would have implicated Derneforde, and therefore Roches, in what might appear to be a treasonable transaction but would, in fact, have been just an intelligent way of dealing with a dangerous situation and protecting English interests. It seems, however, that the evidence was not presented thus at the time and we will probably never know.

It is a matter of record that, by 1386, two or more generations of Dartmouth privateers had haunted the waters around Pointe St Mathieu but even the most cursory glance at that rocky promontory suggests that no sensible seaman would voluntarily linger there for long. Reference was sometimes made to the 'town' of St Mathieu, although none such is recorded as having existed. The small port of Le Conquet to the north of the headland would have provided adequate shelter and a later reference to a ship seized by a '*Blak barge*' of Dartmouth at "*Blanksable in Brittany by the town of Ste. Matthieu*"[57], seems to have been a reference to the mile-long white sand beach,

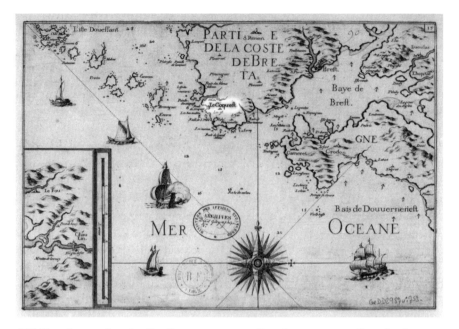

Old French map showing Le Conquet commanding the entrance to Brest harbour.
Atlas des côtes de la France en 1634. Courtesy www.carteanciennes.free.fr

Privateer Lair – Le Conquet with Les Blancs Sablons in the background.
Courtesy www.shelter-invest.com

now known as Les Blancs Sablons, nearby. Another suitable privateer lair can be found in the bay three miles to the east of the cape, where stands the modern town of Plougonvelin. The western side of the bay offers a safe anchorage in most conditions and the gently shoaling, flat, sandy beaches would have been ideal for the beaching of ships when necessary. It also commands the entrance into Brest and beyond; the strait across to the Crozon peninsula being no more than five miles wide at this point. Le Conquet, however, may have been easier to defend from the landward side and, all in all, it seems most likely that Perkyn Dobyn used this small harbour as the base for Hawley's cog *Trinity*, the '*barge of Mortrigo*' and his other vessels in 1385-7[*]. Hawley's ships formed a regular core of the Dartmouth privateering squadron there and sometimes, as seen in the incident with the crayers at Audierne, joined forces with ships from other ports.

Dartmouth seamen still had, by reason of the fight of 1264, historically bad relations with their counterparts at Lyme, but had often collaborated with those of Portsmouth, with whom they reportedly annihilated a French fleet in early 1383 and, later the same year, launched a concerted raid on the Seine in which they destroyed four ships, and captured four others, laden with wine and iron. So it seems that their activities were not restricted to the waters off Brittany, but they generally kept to the west of Cherbourg and the number of claims made against Dartmouth owners and masters in respect of activity in that area suggests that St Mathieu was their home-from-home during the final years of regular privateering activity in the fourteenth century. They were certainly there in some numbers in 1385 when they preyed, apparently indiscriminately, upon Italian, Flemish and even English merchants. It was the Genoese, however, who fell foul of them most often.

In January 1386, no fewer than eight Dartmouth vessels were cited, among others, in a complaint by Genoese merchants based in London, in respect of the 'spoiling' of one of their ships driven ashore on the Breton coast[58]. The Genoese merchants quickly filed suit against John Hawley, along with Hugh Weston, Michael Kykard and others, and the fact that they were at the time making sizeable loans to the English Crown no doubt helped them to secure an order for restitution. The enforcement of the order, however, was another matter. The plundered goods had been scattered far and wide and responsibility for their recovery was placed in the hands of local officials including, of course, John Hawley.

Details of privateering actions in the latter part of the 1380s are sparse but it is recorded in November 1387 that Hawley had, on behalf of himself and sixteen other men of Dartmouth and Kingswear, recompensed two Dutch merchants to the tune of twenty-one tuns of wine, plus damages, in respect of a cargo captured at sea, suggesting that operations were proceeding largely as normal[59]. The Dutch seem to have been regular

---

[*] *Le Conquet is known to have borne that name in 1341 and frequently appears as such in references in the Patent Rolls, but the Dartmouth seamen may have referred to it by its location. As such, it seems probable that Le Conquet was "…the town of Ste Matthieu"*

targets of attacks at this time and, for reasons which remain unclear, it seems that their goods were not always restored to them by the admiralty courts. One nineteenth century historian suggests that 'a merchant of Dartmouth' in 1389 assembled, at his own expense, a fleet of Portuguese ships which captured thirty-four ships carrying fifteen hundred tuns of Rochelle wine.[60] The profits derived from the capture of what must have been an entire wine convoy must have been fabulous and, if this happened, it was a huge enterprise and Hawley was the only Dartmouth merchant who could conceivably have carried it out. Certainly he alone was summoned, and duly appeared in person, before the King's Council in May 1389, to answer what were clearly substantial, although in the record undefined, charges laid by 'men of the king's friendship' in relation to 'undue capture at sea' of a number of Dutch vessels[61]. Hawley was acquitted on this occasion and the courts seem generally to have looked favourably on him in cases brought at this time. He was clearly not regarded by the various officers of the Crown as a pirate and, given the continued parlous state of the maritime defences of Richard's realm, he was the kind of resourceful and determined local leader with whom they needed to do business.

The other Dartmouth burgesses who met Chaucer in 1373 had by now either disappeared from the scene or were active under Hawley's increasingly manifest leadership and, in this light, we can see the latter half of the 1380s as the period when Hawley transformed himself from mere wealthy merchant and comparatively minor privateer-by-proxy into the *de facto* admiral for paranaval activity in the Western Approaches, with Dartmouth as his undisputed power base. He was mayor in 1386, 1388 and 1389 and it is evident that he established his influential position whilst seldom, if ever, going to sea in person. He was to go to sea again in the last years of his life, but at this time he clearly spent more time with his clerks, in the various courts and on horseback than on the decks of his cogs and balingers.

Chapter Five:

Oligarchy & Havoc

The Oligarch: 1388-1402

Admiral Jean de Vienne continued to pose a threat to the fragmented, *ad hoc* maritime defences of Richard II. In 1387, he assembled an invasion fleet at Harfleur and this effort was only frustrated for reasons which had little or nothing to do with English preparedness[*]. There remained a real threat of invasion and the ascendancy of French naval power was such that the king was naturally anxious to support, and to enlist the support of, those who had proven themselves capable of effective action in defending against this kind of danger, by whatever means.

The shipowners of Dartmouth, and Hawley in particular, thus found themselves basking in an official favour born of necessity; the niceties of maritime law in respect of unchecked privateering and plunder having become subordinated to a more pressing exigency. Hawley was soon to prove that he had both the resources and the inclination to take full advantage of the situation, missing no opportunity to increase his personal wealth and influence.

The influence of the Dartmouth burgesses – and of Hawley in particular – now began to extend well beyond the town and its hinterland. On September 2nd 1388, Hawley was appointed collector of customs for the whole of the peninsula, from Melcombe (Weymouth) to Bridgwater, at a rate of three shillings per tun of wine and five per cent of the value of other merchandise, with the exception of raw wool products, from the eve of the preceding Whitsunday (which, in 1388, fell on May 16th) till Trinity of the following year (June 11th)[62]. This 'farm' he purchased for the substantial sum of five hundred pounds, under the condition that he delivered the cash within twelve days. It seems that he missed this demanding deadline but the payment was recorded on September 22nd[63].

---

[*] *Its commander, Olivier de Clisson, was arrested by the duke of Brittany in part of a long-running feud.*

This transaction is interesting in several ways. In the first place, it indicates just how straitened the finances of Richard II had become. The territory in which the 'subsidy' was payable was very extensive and, although Hawley would have incurred significant costs in collecting his dues, the potential net receipts must surely have been considerably more than his five-hundred-pound investment and thus represented a considerable surrender, on the part of the Crown, of future revenue in return for ready cash. That part of his entitlement was in respect of a period of three and a half months which had already passed reflects the fact that farm had been granted, in March 1388, to Richard Bozoun of Exeter, with Hawley's friends, Thomas Asshenden and Benedict de Bottesana, named as collectors[64], and that Hawley was, for some reason, taking it over. It also suggests that his confidence in his ability to collect exceeded that of the officers of the Crown, and that this ability extended well beyond his obvious power base in Dartmouth. The terms of the deal contrast the position of Hawley, who could raise a huge sum of cash in a few days and who clearly believed that his writ would run anywhere along the entire coastline of the south-west, and that of the Crown, whose willingness to treat on such terms indicates a very feeble grip on both its fiscal and administrative affairs. This may also give a clue to a darker side of Hawley's *modus operandi*. It was not unusual for those purchasing tax farms at this time to be unscrupulous and brutal in collecting their dues and, if so inclined, Hawley would, through his privateering acquaintances, have had easy access to the kind of muscle required.

In this light, we can see why the official treatment of Dartmouth at this time of emergency combined quite demanding and onerous commissions with conciliatory gestures and bribes. To John Hawley, the message was that, although he had already done sterling service to the realm, much more was now asked. This was apparent in 1388 when on October 8th, the king ordered the mayor and burgesses of Dartmouth to…:

> "…*contribute to the building of a fortalice by the sea at the entrance of that port, unduly sparing none, and from time to time certifying the King and council of the names of any that rebel: as in consideration of the hurt and peril which might happen to the town in this war by assault of the enemy, the mayor and bailiffs and certain good and able burgesses have purposed to build the same for defence of the town and parts adjacent and of ships of other ports of the realm which touch there…and now the King is informed that a few individuals, scheming to bring there intent to nought, refuse to contribute, and are procuring others to refuse, delaying the work, which manifestly concerns the common weal…*".[65]

Just five weeks later, Hawley was able to obtain letters patent giving the exemption for life…:

> "…*of John Hauley of Dertemuth from being put on assizes, juries, inquisitions or the like and from being made mayor, sheriff, escheator, coroner, collector of tenths or fifteenths or other subsidies or tallages, justice of the peace or of labourers, leader of men at arms, hobelers or archers or other officer or minister of the King, against his will.*"[66]

It is apparent from the language of these two orders that Hawley had been the primary instigator of the project to build the castle but that he had met with some resistance locally and had asked that the order be made. His exemption from undertaking official duties against his will marks his admission to an elite group with whose members there was an implicit bargain under which they would do what they thought was necessary but would not be compelled to undertake offices which they considered to be unnecessary or cumbersome. This is evidenced by the fact that he did subsequently perform several of the roles listed with apparent enthusiasm. In all, the evidence speaks of a man whose position in the town and the surrounding area was now unassailable and who was being given royal sanction to run the show as he thought fit.

Diplomatic initiatives and the death of a number of the advocates of the war on both sides combined with a general war-weariness to give rise to a truce between England and France on June 18th 1389 and this was extended at Leulingham in 1393. The truce, as it turned out, held for more than a decade but, at the time when the construction of the fortalice was commissioned, there was little confidence in it. Even in the anxious years of the late 1380s, however, it is easy to see why the fortalice project may have been controversial locally. There was no suggestion that any central funding would be forthcoming and it was clear that the burden would fall entirely on the local taxpayers. Hawley's stake in the town was by now so substantial that it might be said that what was good for Dartmouth was good for Hawley, and vice versa, but he nonetheless stood to benefit more than anyone else from its protection. Others may well have resented his high-handed assumption that all would contribute to the enterprise, or may simply have felt unable to afford the levies which castle-building, an expensive undertaking by any standards, would imply. It is also likely that some may have questioned its usefulness as anything other than a lookout. The site is at a remove of a mile or so from the town and, although a subsequent fortification there did mount artillery, the guns of Hawley's time, even had they been available to him, would have been of little use in protecting the harbour entrance. Nor, being away from the town itself, would it have been of much use as a redoubt or a keep. There is sketchy evidence of a fortified dwelling at Godmerock, directly opposite on the Kingswear shore, and it would have been possible severely to obstruct entry to the haven by enemy vessels by drawing a boom or chain across the river between the two, although there is no evidence of this having been a part of the scheme at the time.

It is not clear how the construction of the fortalice proceeded or when it was completed. There is an undated petition from some of the burgesses of Dartmouth, complaining of the high cost of building a fortification which was started before the truce. However, completed it was, presumably during the truce, and the remains of its substantial curtain wall and mural towers can still be seen today.

However reluctant some of the burgesses may have been to contribute to the defence of the town and the realm, substantial official recompense was soon forthcoming. On December 2nd 1390, the Patent Rolls show:

*Hawley's fortalice was a controversial project at the time of its construction. This artist's
reconstruction is based on available evidence and was originally drawn by James Stewart
for 'Hawley's Fortalice' by Terry Edwards (Dartmouth History Research Group).*
©James Stewart 1998 www.jamesstewartart.com

"*Grant for three years, to the men of Dertemuth, which above other places in the realm has long
been and still is strong in shipping and therewith has brought great havoc on the King's enemies
in time of war, that the export of tin to foreign parts shall be from Dertemuth and from nowhere
else provided always that previous to export the tin be duly weighted and customed.*"[67]

Although monopolies of this kind must, overall, have had a deleterious effect on the
trades to which they related, it was not unusual for such to be awarded for pragmatic
political reasons and, in this case, the reason was explicitly given. Of the Stannary towns
of Truro, Lostwithiel, Launceston and Helston in Cornwall and Tavistock, Plympton,
Chagford and Ashburton in Devon, only Ashburton, being seven miles or so from the

navigable head of the Dart, might logically have used Dartmouth as a port. Lostwithiel, which had been the principal port for tin exports since it was established as such in Norman times, may have lost its pre-eminence, as the effluent from the very tin workings that it served silted up the river but, lying just five miles or so from the Fowey estuary, it still held considerable natural advantages over Dartmouth. If account is taken of the inconvenience thus imposed on the tinners of the Stannary towns, the extent of the favour granted to the Dartmouth men at their expense can be appreciated. This piece of pure political patronage would certainly have brought substantial, if transient, benefits to Dartmouth but was otherwise nonsensical. The benefits to Dartmouth, if there ever were any, proved to be very short-lived indeed, as the predictable protests were soon forthcoming. The Lostwithiel tinners petitioned Parliament in November 1391:

> "...the commons pray that whereas in Cornwall there accrues a great commodity of the kingdom of England, that is tin, which has been greatly damaged by the statute and ordinances made in the last parliament held at Westminster, namely that the staple of the same tin should be at Dartmouth, to which place it does not please the merchants to come to buy the said tin and also, that neither the English merchants nor others can take nor transport the said tin overseas, nor to any other part, until they have brought the said tin to the aforesaid Dartmouth, to the great cost and ruin of the said lieges, and to the great injury and debasement of the coinage of our lord the king. May it please you to ordain that the aforesaid ordinances and statute be annulled, and that the said lieges, and all other merchants repairing to the said realm, be permitted to take the said tin wherever they will, as well overseas as on this side of the sea, paying the customs due thereon. And that the staple of the said tin be at Lostwithiel in the aforesaid county."[68]

They soon, within the same parliament, received what at first looked like a favourable response:

> "The king wills that the said ordinances and statute be annulled: and that between now and the feast of St John the Baptist next [24th June 1392] denizens and aliens be free to load tin into ships and other vessels to be taken out of the kingdom from whatsoever port they choose in the kingdom, and to wheresoever they will."

The sting, however, was in the tail:

> "And after the said feast they shall repair to Calais, for the time when the return of wool shall be there, paying always the dues, customs and subsidies owed thereon before the passage of the aforesaid tin."[69]

The Dartmouth monopoly, in other words, had been revoked but the staple had been moved not back to Lostwithiel but to Calais. The response was rational and

A romanticised depiction of the death of Robert Tresilian – He was in fact dragged, fighting, to Tyburn Tree, where he was hanged naked and his throat cut.

Illustration from a manuscript of Froissart's Chronicles c 1470

balanced but it was not what either the men of Lostwithiel, or of Dartmouth, had wanted.

John Hawley's fortunes were clearly in the ascendant at this time but, if the uncertainties and febrile politics of the late 1380s played well for him, the same could not be said for Robert Tresilian. Sir Robert, a career lawyer, was from a landed Cornish family of the eponymous manor of Tresillian, near Truro. He entered the service of the king and was knighted and appointed a justice of the King's Bench in 1378. When Sir John Cavendish, Chief Justice of the King's Bench, was killed during the Peasants' Revolt of 1381, Tresilian was appointed as his successor and immediately, in his conduct of the trials of the rebels, displayed a brutality and lack of scruple for which he was to become notorious. His position thus established, he behaved opportunistically in the shifting, partisan politics of the next decade, infamously dispensing justice in whatever manner he perceived to serve the immediate interests of the king. Such were his excesses that he became one of the main targets of the ire of five noblemen who were to become known as the Lords Appellant and who, in November 1387, challenged the authority of the king's henchmen, and thus the king himself.

Although the Appellants did not seek to depose Richard, their actions were tantamount to a *coup d'état* and the king was effectively held prisoner while the so-called Merciless Parliament meted out punishment to those deemed guilty of subverting the governance of the nation. Tresilian, one of the most loathed of the royal henchmen, fled but was convicted *in absentia* of giving 'aid and counsel' to traitors and sentenced to death on February 13th 1388. He was discovered, six days later, hiding under a table in Westminster, disguised in strange clothes and, allegedly, a false beard. He was quickly recognised because of his distinctive and well-known voice, dragged out to cries of *"We havet hym"*, and brought before parliament. His claims for sanctuary and of a mistrial were quickly dismissed and he was drawn on a hurdle to Tyburn. He was physically forced to mount the scaffold and his clothes, which were found to be filled with protective charms, were stripped from him. He was hanged naked and his throat was cut.[70]

Tresilian's wife, Emmaline, who had married him as a widow in 1377, reportedly screamed and fainted when he was arrested, but regained her composure sufficiently, within a year or two, to marry Sir John Colshull, surviving until 1403. Her ability to make yet another good marriage in such circumstances suggests that, having been of landed wealth in her own right, she had managed to salvage significant assets when those of her late husband were seized.

It was at this point that the paths of the Tresilian and Hawley families crossed. Whatever the king's personal views on the fate of his late, close ally may have been, Tresilian had been executed for a serious crime and his lands and property were therefore forfeit to the Crown. This provided the cash-rich Hawley with a rare opportunity to acquire substantial estates, albeit at some remove from his home base. His first acquisition, for a consideration of two hundred and twenty marks*, was in July 1389, but a purchase recorded on November 23rd of that year gives a better flavour of the extent to which he was becoming a member of the landed gentry:

> *"Grant with the assent of the Great Council, for 820 marks paid to John de Hermesthorpe for the King's use by John Hauley of Dertemuth, to him, his heirs etc. as from Michaelmas last, of the manors of Lametton, Tresilian, Boseveynon, Rageney, Kilmynauth and Trenewyth with their appurtenances and certain lands and tenements in Bre, Hendre, and Hesenefordmyll, the avowson of Lametton, all lands and tenements, rents and services and two tinworks at Bourdanos, Crukbergus and all other tinworks within the precincts of the said manors, late of Robert Tresilian, knight, forfeited by virtue of the judgment against him in the late Parliament at Westminster."[71]*

A similar transaction, for a consideration of forty pounds, was made in May the following year, extending Hawley's holdings to the Scillies and to Duloe, near Looe. His purchases of Cornish lands later extended beyond those forfeit to the Crown by Tresilian when, in 1393, he bought a lease *"for the term of the life of Emma, wife of John Colshull"* on two manors, three dwellings and twenty acres of land, these being, presumably, the parts of the Tresilian estate which Emmaline had brought to that marriage and now wished to dispose of[72]. These properties were mostly clustered around Truro and Camborne, the latter, interestingly, giving Hawley a significant interest in tin mining[†], but the advowson[‡] of 'Lammeton' presumably refers to Lamerton near Tavistock. The transactions with Emmaline and her new husband were not, however, all one-way. In May 1394 we see Hawley exchanging with them four dwellings and twenty-four acres in Duloe, which he had acquired as part of the 1390 purchase, for the manor and advowson of East Washbourne in Devon, perhaps in an effort to tidy up his holdings[73].

---

* *A mark was a unit of account which was generally accepted in Europe as equivalent to eight ounces of silver. In England, it signified 13s.4d. or two-thirds of a pound Sterling.*

† *Hawley's role as escheator also brought him into contact with mining. In August 1391 he was, among other commissioners, instructed to "...survey the newly found mines of gold, silver, lead, tin and other metals in [Devon and Cornwall], set the necessary workmen and labourers to work for the King's advantage..."*

‡ *The right to appoint a new Rector to a parish in the event that the living falls vacant.*

Hawley handled the transactions which elevated him to the status of a landed gentleman with his characteristic shrewdness, but the process was not entirely straightforward. In November 1393 he felt obliged to seek an injunction against *"divers lieges"* – gangs of armed peasants – who had occupied some of his Cornish lands and *"...assaulted his men and servants in collecting arrears of rent...threatened to kill them and besieged them for a long time at Mousehole".*[74] From the outset, some of the former Tresilian tenants had opposed the deal and Tresilian's son, John, eventually persuaded the king to overturn it and to grant him full rights to his claimed inheritance.

Hawley had taken the precaution, when purchasing the lands from the Crown, of including a clause that, if he or his heirs in title were ever evicted from the property, the Crown would be obliged to make good the loss. In the event, however, he did not need to seek recourse to this provision, as the setback proved to be temporary. Richard II's June 1399 ruling in favour of John Tresilian, with whose cause he perhaps had some residual sympathy, turned out to be one of the last acts of his troubled reign as, at the end of that month, Henry Bolingbroke, duke of Lancaster, sailed from Boulogne to begin the short campaign which was to lead to Richard's overthrow. At the end of September, he was forced to resign the crown and five months later he was dead. In November 1399, Henry IV confirmed Hawley's letters patent, reinforcing his title.

Hawley's involvement with Tresilian's estate and surviving family are known to have extended for over ten years. It was customary for the orphaned heirs of the king's tenants to be made wards of suitable guardians, most of whom had no connection with their families. In reality, because the guardianship often brought with it significant rents or other revenues, these were either commercial transactions or represented royal patronage to the guardians.* Such arrangements usually lasted for the period of the ward's minority or until they married, but the contract into which John Hawley and his son entered in February 1402 was somewhat different. They purchased the wardship and *"...custody of all lands pertaining to him* [the grantor – in this case Henry of Monmouth, Prince of Wales] *by reason of the idiocy of Elizabeth Tresylian daughter of Robert Tresylian, deceased, and of her body etc. for 13s. 4d. paid in the hanaper*†*."*[75] The contract further required that the Hawleys make suitable provision for Elizabeth's care and that half of the income from the estate would accrue to the prince. It may be assumed, however, that Elizabeth was, by 1402, no longer a minor and that her "idiocy" made her unmarriageable and so the residual portion of the revenues from whatever lands and property were settled upon her from her father's estate would continue to pass to the Hawleys, father and son, until her death – a considerable annuity against an outlay of thirteen shillings and fourpence. This consideration probably explains why Hawley took care that both he and his son were parties to the transaction

---

* *Chaucer benefited from such arrangements, one of which – the wardship of Edmund Staplegate – brought him the handsome sum of £104 in 1375.*

† *An office of the Chancery Court – originally a reference to a basket (hamper) into which writs were placed.*

This much of the Hawley-Tresilian connection is clear. Historians over the years have, however, persisted in suggesting that the two families also became connected by marriage. Various theories as to the nature of this link have been advanced; some are broadly plausible but none is supported by any direct evidence. Tresilian is believed to have had, by Emmaline, a son, John, and at least four daughters – Joan, Emma, Margaret and Elizabeth. It has been stated as fact by some writers that Emma (or Emmaline) was the second wife of the second John Hawley, in spite of the clear evidence that Hawley's second wife was named Alicia or Alice. Another suggests that Emma(line), the daughter, married the younger John Hawley, although his wife is known to have been called Margaret. No less an authority than the *Dictionary of National Biography* suggests that Joan Tresilian and Joan, the first wife of the second John Hawley may have been one and the same. Joan first appears as Hawley's wife in 1372, and although her age is unknown, it is just possible that she might have been a daughter of Tresilian. However, there is no known connection between Hawley and Tresilian prior to that date and Joan, in its various forms, was a very common name at the time. As such, the idea is not very persuasive.

Historians may feel compelled to make speculations of this nature because the period produced many pragmatic marriage alliances and the theories seem fitting in that sense. The marriage of heiresses was a routine means by which the gentry expanded their land holdings and thus elevated their status but, however attractive the potential inheritances of Tresilian's daughters may have been, at the time of his marriage to Joan, Hawley was still some way from making his bid for the status of landed gentleman or esquire and it seems far more likely that, like his friend Thomas Asshenden, he had followed the more normal practice of marrying within the merchant class. The paucity of information on the wives of the elder and younger Hawleys certainly engenders a desire speculatively to fill in the gaps but, of Joan and Margaret we know very little and of Alice, apart from the date of her death in 1403, nothing at all. Joan died on July 12th 1394 and it is not known when Hawley married Alice. Although it probably came fairly soon after Joan's death, there is no specific evidence to suggest that the marriage with Alice was a strategic one.

A more plausible theory of a link by marriage, although it is again one which is backed by no hard evidence, is that Margaret, the wife of the younger John Hawley, may have been Tresilian's daughter of that name. Margaret Tresilian had been married in 1386 to Sir John Arundell of Lanherne, who had been a ward of her father in his minority.[76] With Tresilian's downfall in 1388, Arundell divorced her and, if the Hawleys had no feelings of political squeamishness about her treasonable parentage, such a marriage may indeed have made sense to both parties. Margaret would also have been about the right age to marry the younger John Hawley, but it is impossible to link the dates of Margaret Tresilian's divorce from Arundell in 1388 with John's marriage to his Margaret, which is only known to have occurred sometime before the couple's first appearance in the ecclesiastical records in June 1408. In the absence of any other or specific evidence that there was a connection between the two families by marriage, it may be unreasonable to infer that there was such a link simply because they were known, over the years, to have had dealings and because of coincidences of some very common Christian names.*

In the last years of the reign of Richard II, Hawley consolidated his position as the foremost among the local oligarchs and, his exemptions from obligatory public office notwithstanding, involved himself in a variety of official and private non-maritime activities. He held various public offices in the early 1390s, including that of escheator†, a role made accessible to him by his new status as a landowner. Complaints recorded in actions against him during this period suggest that he did not always discharge these duties fully or efficiently and there was at least one claim that he had not done so honestly, but such criticism of officials was quite normal and may not be a meaningful reflection on his performance. Given the wide range of his commitments, however, it would not be surprising if he was at least occasionally guilty of neglect. In any event, his star was in the ascendant and his elevation to armigerous rank came on May 16th 1395 when the king granted his "esquire" John Hawley an annuity of forty marks for life[77]. By the values of the rigid social hierarchy of late medieval England, this marked the pinnacle of his career.

Image of John Corp's father and deceased daughter, Elianore, for whom his balinger may have been named – in St Peter's church, Stoke Fleming.
Courtesy of William Lack, H Martin Stuchfield and Philip Whittemore, The Monumental Brasses of Devonshire (2000)

Hawley's service to the Crown at this time extended to the transportation of royal personages. There is direct evidence of a connection with this kind of activity in the gift by Hawley and Thomas Knapp of Bristol of two *"great masts and all the ankers and accessories for a King's ship"* in 1396, just prior to Richard's journey to Calais, amid much pomp and ceremony, to marry Isabella, the seven year-old daughter of the king

---

* Dorothy Gardiner suggests that, had there been any relationship between the Tresilians and the Hawleys by marriage, the fact would have been mentioned in the wardship papers for Elizabeth. It was not. This absence might be explained if the younger John married Margaret Tresilian after 1402, which was already fourteen years after her divorce. This seems unlikely.

† An officer of the office of Escheator General who dealt with lands which reverted to their original grantor or to the Crown, because the owner died without heir or, by reason of being convicted of a serious crime, was debarred from bequeathing them.

of France.* Richard's entourage on this occasion exceeded five hundred people, plus their horses and baggage and, although it was in the *Elianore*†, a balinger owned by another Dartmouth man, John Corp, that the king and his immediate entourage sailed, two of Hawley's ships, the *Margret* and the *Petre*, joined the supporting flotilla. It is likely that one or more special ships were fitted out to convey the retinue in suitable style and the masts were perhaps for this purpose – gifts from loyal and well-heeled subjects to the king in celebration of the happy event.

Whatever its specific purpose, the gift suggests that Knapp and Hawley were assiduously cultivating their relationships with the monarch and his court. Knapp, Bristol's leading shipowner, may have had more particular reasons for doing so because, when serving as MP for Bristol in the Merciless Parliament of 1388 his name had been associated with the cause of the Lords Appellant, against whom Richard subsequently took revenge. Certainly he joined with three other Bristol merchants in lending two hundred pounds to the king in 1396 and sought a royal pardon in 1398.

There was little scope for privateering during the ten-year truce with France, but Dartmouth seems to have continued to prosper nonetheless. Again the port's ships turned to more peaceable activities and, as in the truce of the 1360s, it seems that they were involved in a logistical capacity in the king's service. There is clear evidence of this from Hawley's request that witnesses in the case of Roches vs. Hawley be allowed to give sworn testimonies in Dartmouth because it was difficult to bring them to Westminster, by reason of their being employed in the king's service in Ireland or in France; the implication being that this was in his own ships and that the witnesses could only be called when they returned to their home port.

In addition to this kind of official business, there are records in the 1390s of ships embarking pilgrims to the shrine of St James of Compostella, with ships masters' being given licence to take eighty or a hundred passengers in order that they could make their vows, and to bring them back. It is likely that they sailed to Coruña, the nearest port to Santiago, and, for non-seafaring pilgrims crammed into a 14th Century cog, the habitually bumpy conditions of the long haul across the Bay of Biscay likely provided an added element of spiritual purgation. For the Dartmouth seamen, however, this and other unfamiliar peacetime activities helped to create some semblance of business as usual and it is in this connection that Hawley's old friend Thomas Asshenden made his final appearance in the official record when, in April 1391, he obtained:

---

* *The Customs accounts for 1396 indicate that floating the two masts down the Dart cost 4s.5d.(a figure which Russell (op.cit.) equates with fourteen man days' labour) but the whole cost of taking the masts and rigging to Greenwich amounted to £16.12s.11d. This cost included a pipe of cider (6s.8d.) and a barrel of ale (3s.) for the mariners and £8 for their wages. The second largest expense item, interestingly, was £7.10s. for rope. (See Michell Whitley op.cit. p.532.)*

† *Most ships of the time bore the names of saints but Corp may, endearingly, have named this vessel for his late daughter, who had died in 1391 and whose effigy can be seen, together with that of his father, in the parish church in Stoke Fleming.*

Westminster Hall – scene of a turbulent assembly in Hawley's time.
Courtesy Project Gutenberg

> "Licence for the king's liege Thomas Asshendon, of Dertemuth to, ship in a vessel
> of that town two hundred of the king's lieges as pilgrims to Santiago in Spain,
> whereof he may make proclamation throughout the realm, paying custom and
> other dues to the king's use, but the pilgrims must not carry gold or silver, in
> bullion or money, or other things contrary to statute."[78]

During the ten-year truce with France, Hawley appears to have settled into the
longest period of near-normal life that he ever enjoyed. Life for Hawley was, of course,
never entirely uneventful and, in addition to the death of Joan in 1394 and his marriage
to Alicia, the case of Roches v. Hawley rumbled on. The borough, manor, naval and
commercial records relating to Dartmouth during the truce of the 1390s portray, for
the most part, a routine domesticity in which he played his customary, frenetic role. He
served as mayor in 1391, 1393, 1394, 1395, 1398 and 1399 and presided over the various
contracts and disputes of a prosperous port. However, while an uneasy truce prevailed in
the Western Approaches and life in Dartmouth was largely peaceful, trouble was never
far below the surface of English politics as a whole and Hawley, as an MP for Dartmouth
in 1390, 1393, 1394 and 1402, had a ringside seat.

Although the now fifty year-old Hawley was perhaps as well prepared by nature and
experience as anyone for the cut-and-thrust and intrigue of Westminster politics and influence
broking, we can imagine that he would have been glad to be accompanied on his first visit to
that turbulent assembly by Thomas Asshenden, who had already attended three parliaments
and would have been able to show his fellow mariner the ropes. The pair attended the first of
the two Parliaments to be called in 1390, which sat from January 17th until March 2nd.

The Commons of the 1390s was still far from the supreme deliberative and legislative body that it was later to become and, whilst its assent to proposals coming from the court and the lords was deemed necessary in order to maintain England's social cohesion, the initiative on matters of national policy seldom if ever came from the local MPs, whose interests were often purely parochial. Devon was represented at Hawley's first Parliament in January 1390 by a total of sixteen members: Sir Philip Courtenay, earl of Devon, and Sir James Chudleigh, a landowner and professional soldier, together with two representatives from each of Ashburton, Barnstaple, Dartmouth, Exeter, Plympton Erle, Tavistock and Totnes. The long experience of Hawley and Asshenden in defence and paranaval activities and the administration of a small but complex borough would have enabled them to comment intelligently on a wider range of issues than could many of their fellow MPs, but the elected members of the Commons tended to defer to the feudal hierarchy in most matters of diplomacy and national politics and it is likely that, if they had wished to make representations with regard to such matters, they would have done so through Courtenay and Chudleigh.

The merchant classes did sometimes present written petitions requesting intercession with the king 'in the name of the Commons' with regard to their more local or personal interests and Hawley and Asshenden perhaps heard such a petition in 1390 – from merchants exporting cloth made in Somerset, Dorset, Bristol and Gloucestershire, claiming that they had been sold fabrics which were badly dyed or woven fabrics or otherwise of inferior quality, which had been deceitfully rolled inside good cloth, and requesting intervention on their behalf.

A topic that was always close to the hearts of the Commons, and one on which it was particularly important for the king to receive their willing assent, was taxation. A nation accustomed to war had also become somewhat inured to the levels of taxation necessary to sustain it, but it was, of course, never welcome. On March 1st 1390, Hawley, Asshenden and the others voted, in view of the prevailing truce, to reduce the poundage levy on general merchandise trade by half. This, at least, would have been a subject on which the Dartmothians had clear views.

As a result of a quarrel between Richard II and the City of London, apparently because of the latter's having, unusually, refused a request from the Crown for a loan of £10,000, the parliament of 1393 was summoned to attend the king at Winchester*. Hawley therefore had less far to travel to the parliament which, on January 20th assembled and awaited the somewhat delayed arrival of the king at Wolvesey Palace, the residence of the Bishop of Winchester. In the great hall of that palace, as at Westminster in 1390, he witnessed debates on issues regarding which he had no reason to have any particular knowledge or interest. The principal focus of discussions and legislation at this parliament was the desire of the English king and aristocracy to limit the ability of the papacy to intervene in

---

* On this occasion, he was accompanied by John Ellemede, a lawyer from Tiverton who had little contact with the Dartmouth burgesses but lived in Cornworthy and was probably elected on the strength of his legal credentials.

domestic affairs. If, however, our gritty privateer found these arcane proceedings boring, he may at least have found some diversion in an incident which occurred there, involving Sir Philip Courtenay, an uncle of the earl of Devon. Courtenay was attending as an elected knight of the shire but, on the first day of the session, he:

> "...came before the king in full parliament saying that he had heard that certain men had accused and slandered him to the king and lords, as well by bill as by word of mouth, of heinous matters; whereupon he prayed to be discharged of the said occupation until the said accusation and complaints had been tried and found true or false."[79]

Courtenay had found himself confronted at Winchester by two of his neighbours, Nicholas Potingdon and Richard Somerset, who had pursued him from Devon and submitted a petition claiming that he had forcibly ejected them from their lands there and that he was *"so great in his country that no poor man dares to pursue the law against him, nor to tell the truth against him in the same county"*. These accusations were deemed to be sufficiently serious that Courtenay was temporarily excused his duties while the matter was investigated. On the following Monday, however, and having *"consented to a good truce"*, he was restored, in full parliament, *"to his good repute"*.

At the Parliament which sat at Westminster from January 27th until March 6th 1394, Hawley was accompanied by William Damiet, another privateering captain who lived in Kingswear and who was to become mayor of Dartmouth in 1397. Hawley likely found the trip to London more pleasant for Damiet's companionship but he may have been less comfortable if, in the mêlée in Westminster Hall, he sometimes found himself face to face with that knight of the Shire representing Wiltshire, Sir John de Roches. The two men were both in attendance at the Parliament of 1394, while their legal confrontation continued at the same venue.

On this occasion, the two Dartmouth mariners, together with their fellow commoners, were asked to deliberate on a matter of high politics. The Commons were charged to give their 'advice and counsel' with regard to parts of an agreement previously drawn up between the king and Charles VI of France which might form the basis of a peace treaty between the two realms. They did discuss this and passed their advice, such as it was, through the Speaker, Sir John Bussy. They opined that, as the three central issues of liege homage, sovereignty and judicial appeal were beyond their competence to give counsel, they would defer to the king and the Lords. They were then relieved of the obligation to advise on the matter.

If the elected members of the Commons lacked influence on most of the major issues of national and international politics, they were accordingly able, for the most part, to keep their heads below the parapet when political upheaval imperilled their knightly and aristocratic betters. There is no record of Dartmouth being represented at all at the turbulent parliaments of 1398 and 1399 which preceded the overthrow of Richard II and so Hawley probably missed the worst of the action. The accession of Henry IV to the throne was marked by the kind of factional bloodletting which so often accompanied regime change in the late Middle Ages and, among others, Sir John Bussy, who had presided as Speaker over all of Hawley's parliaments so far, was deposed and beheaded. Although Hawley had worked hard to cultivate a good relationship with Richard's court, he had displayed no more than the obsequiousness required by protocol and self-interest and so the new regime had no reason to suspect or persecute him. In fact, having recently lost his Cornish lands to John Tresilian at the behest of Richard, it is likely that he welcomed Henry's *coup d'état*. As we have seen, he was soon to benefit from it, when Henry restored the lands to him.

Much had changed in the eight years which had passed between Hawley's third attendance at Westminster for the Parliament of 1394 and his fourth and last journey there as MP, for the session which opened on the last day of September 1402. This was the third parliament of Henry IV's reign and it was a fearful monarch who presided over it. On October 2nd Hawley and the others gathered to hear the Chancellor, Edmund Stafford, Bishop of Exeter, deliver the *pronunciato* – the formal declaration of the reasons why the Parliament had been called. The message, delivered in a style of ecclesiastical exhortation, was a mixed one.

Bishop Stafford started by reminding those present that God had sent Henry for the salvation of the realm and that it was He who had delivered their Scottish enemies to them as prisoners. This was a reference to the recent victory of Sir Henry Percy, earl of Northumberland ('Hotspur') over the Scots at Homildon Hill. He also referred to the continuing schism in the Church and said the Holy Roman Emperor had written to Henry, asking him to intercede in the quarrel in his capacity as "*...the most powerful king in the world*" but went on to outline the challenges – in Scotland, Wales, Ireland and France – which confronted this all-powerful monarch. The exhortation, in effect, was that, in spite of all the problems which confronted the realm, the Commons should place their trust in God and Harry.

Henry thus had good reason to be nervous and, on top of it all, he was impecunious. The Commons, however, were not about to sanction large tax increases without investigating what had happened to Richard's treasure after he was deposed and they asked permission to 'inter-commune' with some of the Lords regarding treasury matters – effectively establishing a kind of liaison committee. Henry resisted setting uncomfortable precedents which would limit his powers in future and only granted this facility to this Parliament as a temporary concession, "*...de sa grace especiale*". Temporary or not, the concession proved to be effective as, when they had interrogated John Ikelington, Richard's former clerk, and when the inter-communion with the Lords confirmed what Henry had said – that the funds had all been paid to the Percy family to prosecute the war with the Scots – the Commons reluctantly agreed. On November 25th, the last day of the Parliament, they voted in favour of a renewal of the wool subsidy for another three years and the imposition of a whole tenth and fifteenth for the next twelve months. This was the final act of John Hawley's parliamentary career.

Hawley was now in his early sixties and had been spectacularly successful in every aspect of his career. The riches of trade and plunder continued to flow to Hawley's Hoe, he was of landed wealth, had been elevated to the squirearchy, had a coat of arms and a son who was already giving him reason to believe he would be a worthy heir. He had completed his last term as mayor the previous year, making fourteen terms in all, had served in four parliaments and held several high offices. He had outlived the companions and collaborators of his youth, as well as his first wife. He had outlived both John of Gaunt and Geoffrey Chaucer. He had, so to speak, done it all, and yet, by the time he travelled to Westminster in September

Henry Bolingbroke – King Henry IV of England – reviled by the French as a usurper.

Illustration from Cassell's History of England 1902

1402, he had already begun to apply himself to the protection of the realm and the extension of his controversial life's work with an almost reckless energy which, even in this exceptional man, can only be described as extraordinary. The elderly John Hawley was already causing more trouble to the French than he ever had in his youth.

Wreaking Havoc: 1402-1408

The king of France was mad. Charles VI had suffered bouts of paranoid delusions since 1392 and the duke of Burgundy had assumed the regency. In this capacity, Burgundy was constantly challenged and impeded by Louis of Valois, duke of Orléans. Orléans opposed Burgundy's foreign policy in general and the truce with England in particular. When Richard II confiscated the lands of Henry Bolingbroke and sent him into exile in 1399, Orléans, working on the principle that his enemy's enemy was a potential friend, gave Henry a warm welcome in Paris, where the two seem to have arrived at some kind of pledge of mutual support. On his part, Orléans almost certainly did this for reasons of internal, French politics but he did nothing to prevent Henry from mounting an expedition to recover his inheritance in England. Henry's ambitions were, of course, far larger than that and, within weeks of landing in Yorkshire in July, he had seized control of England. Orléans had got much more than he had bargained for.

Although otherwise riven by factionalism, the ruling classes of France, Orléans included, were united in their horror at this usurpation of the God-given sovereignty of Richard II, the more so because of the affront to Richard's queen, Isabella, a royal daughter of France. Orléans immediately became a sworn enemy of the usurper but French policy in general was more cautious, not least because of Isabella's status as hostage. Henry, meanwhile, had too many problems on other fronts to want an immediate confrontation with France and his reaffirmation of the truce in 1400, together with some foot-dragging in respect of the return of Isabella, won him some breathing space. After refusing to contemplate Henry's suggestion that she might marry his son, the future Henry V, Isabella was allowed to return to France in May 1401. In spite of Henry's efforts to ward off all-out war with France, it was only a matter of time before the uncertain truce broke down. In October 1403, Henry's estranged friend, Orléans, marched on Gascony and the war resumed in the following spring.

The old privateer had been less reticent about a resumption of hostilities than had the young king and Hawley was a prominent figure in the phoney war at sea which developed between 1400 and the formal resumption of hostilities in 1404. Although Henry had been at pains to issue proclamations forbidding attacks on French ships, his financial difficulties prevented him from impressing large official fleets and he was obliged to waive this protection with regard to French and other vessels which were providing assistance to the Welsh and Scottish rebels. Henry's expedition into Scotland in August 1400, with a force of ten or fifteen thousand men, although arguably ill-advised, was real enough and he needed to enlist paranaval support in cutting off the enemy's sources of supply. Hawley's importance to the defence of the south-west and to the prosecution of any war at sea, the blockading of the Scots included, was as obvious to Henry as it had been to Richard and this was given official recognition in his appointment as lieutenant to the Admiral of England, Thomas Percy, earl of Worcester, from 1399 until 1401*. During this period, the southern fleet, under the command of John Hawley and Richard Spicer, was responsible for defending the Channel coast, while the Northern fleet, under John Brandon, William Prince and William Terry, was principally concerned with blockading the Scots. When Henry reaffirmed the truce in June 1400, these fleets were stood down and there were no reports of attacks by English ships on French vessels until March 1401.

In June 1401, Hawley captured at sea a ship under the command of Jean de la Chapelle of Abbeville, giving rise to the customary claims against him. In this instance, his actions seem to have been legitimate because the vessel was bound for Scotland, carrying a cargo of wheat, flour and sailcloth. A quarter of the cargo was the property of two merchants of Bruges, who duly lodged a claim against Hawley. Hawley was, however, by now a past master of this kind of litigation and successfully resisted the claim, pointing out that the Brugeois merchants were in partnership with a Scot, something which they had omitted to mention.

During his brief tenure of this office, we see Hawley acting in the judicial capacity which came with the job. He is cited in June 1401 as having previously given judgement in a maritime case in favour of a chaplain of Exeter and against a Kingsbridge mariner, who subsequently appealed. The poacher was, for the time being, playing gamekeeper but it seems that it was a responsibility which he was able to delegate. In a case cited in an appeal the following November, another Dartmouth man, William Knoll, is named as having substituted for him.

**Dartmouth Museum model
of the** Christopher.

Courtesy of Dartmouth Museum

It is apparent that, while in Westminster for the Parliament of 1402, he did not restrict himself to general parliamentary business and managed to drum up some for himself for, on October 18th 1402, while the Parliament was still in session, we see:

"Commission to John Hauley, John Moor and John Andrewe of Dertemuth, to take mariners for a ship called 'Seinte John Christofer' and a barge called 'Seinte Marie Ship' of the said John Hauley at Dertemuth and thence along the sea coast on one side to Seton and on the other side to Zalme[*], to serve the King on a voyage at sea." [80]

Of all of Hawley's ships, the one whose name is most famously associated with his legend is his great cog *Christopher*. Her name, like that of her owner, appears in various forms and spellings and it does seem that he commanded her in person. She makes her first appearance in the official record in another commission of the same day which shows:

"Among other ships ordered to Southampton are 'le Cristofre' of Dertemouth (140 tuns) of John Hauley; 'le Lythenard' (84 tuns) of Munday Arnald and John Thornyng; 'le George' (67 tuns) of Robert Smyth and John Gerard; 'le Cogge John' (60 tuns) of William Gilberd, Richard Gilberd and John Stephenys" [81]

At a hundred and forty tons, the *Christopher* was a sizeable vessel and it seems that she became the *de facto* flagship of Hawley, the *de facto* admiral of an unofficial fleet. It is noteworthy that, of all the names of shipowners mentioned in this and other commissions and writs of this time, Hawley's is the only one to appear both before and after the truce of the 1390s. As such, we can see why, whether officially appointed or not, his authority in this company would have been unquestioned. The Westcountry privateers, Hawley foremost amongst them, had long been accustomed to assisting the king in naval matters, and to exploiting the legal and political loopholes which the situation provided. Hawley, doubtless emboldened by his various official endorsements and confident that he would be given the benefit of the doubt in marginal cases or that his transgressions would be ignored altogether, was straining at the leash.

---

[*] *Obscure. Zalme has survived as a Flemish/Dutch surname and this is perhaps a reference to some small port around the estuary of the Scheldt.*

Henry's diplomatic efforts to maintain the truce were being met with gradually increasing hostility in France and his proclamations of 1400 were his last attempt to rein in the privateers, to whom the subtleties of his foreign policy must have been incomprehensible. It is also clear that little or no restraint was being exercised on the other side of the Channel, as French attacks on English shipping, some of which were conducted by officers of the French Crown, increased dramatically. If Hawley was playing by the rules when sailing under royal orders, it seems that his French counterparts were not. It is striking that the surviving records of incidents of alleged piracy during this period predominantly refer to ships of Castile and Flanders and not of France. This is almost certainly because the governments on both sides had started to give tacit consent to unlicensed privateering which, in any other circumstances, would have constituted pure piracy, and to use it as an instrument of an undeclared war. In the latter part of 1401 it was becoming increasingly clear that what was to become known as the 'pirate war' was in fact an extension of official policy on both sides.

That is not to say that it was only tacitly sanctioned paranaval activity that was going on. More than half of the actions taken by the English against French vessels in 1401 were explicitly carried out as reprisals and it has been suggested that many of them were the result of what amounted to a private war between the Dartmothians and the merchants of La Rochelle. In all, fifty-two English ships were recorded as having been attacked or captured by the French in 1401 and Henry, realising that the English merchants had no hope of obtaining restitution, ceased trying to give redress to French claimants. On August 3rd of that year, Henry's ambassadors made a last-ditch effort to stabilise the situation and a meeting to discuss the 'piracy' problem was convened, but this achieved nothing of any substance. Subsequently planned meetings were delayed as the French prevaricated and all came to nothing. This was part of a steadily swelling stream of provocation by a French government unwilling to preserve the truce and determined to overthrow Henry the usurper.

Another major element in the French effort to overthrow Henry was their support of the Scots, with whom Henry was fighting a declared war. The Scottish admiral, the earl of Crawford, in January 1402, requested French assistance and signed an alliance with Orléans. A fleet was assembled at Harfleur, ostensibly to escort Crawford home, and this was responsible for the seizure of at least twenty-five of the thirty-three English vessels lost in the Channel during the four months which passed between its departure from that port and its arrival in Scotland. This Franco-Scottish aggression was not, however, to go unopposed. Henry, alerted by the mayor of the Calais staple of the fleet assembling at Harfleur, ordered the southern admiral, Thomas Rempston, to assemble a force in response. Rempston's position as admiral was not a reflection of relevant experience but rather of his status as a long-time, close associate of Henry Bolingbroke. Rempston was no mariner and, as ever, the Crown called upon the privateer captains for assistance. Their response was swift, professional and extremely effective. Hawley assembled a Dartmouth fleet, which was commanded by himself, John Corp, Robert Bolt and Edmund Arnold, while Mark Mixto brought a fleet out of Fowey and Henry Pay and Richard Spicer gathered a flotilla from Southampton. In the absence of an official admiral, these men were often referred to as captains and admirals. While Crawford was at sea with his French allies, the Westcountrymen captured forty-eight French ships, at least eighteen of which fell prey to the Dartmouth men. Once unleashed, they had levelled the score with alacrity.

Relations between England and Brittany were now briefly thrown into confusion by one of the most surprising events of Henry IV's reign. John, duke of Brittany had died in November 1399 and his young widow, Joan of Navarre, was acting as regent. She had probably met Henry IV as early as the wedding of Richard and Isabella in 1396 and again during Henry's exile, and it is evident that there was a strong mutual affection between them. On Brittany's death, she had immediately opened a very cordial correspondence with Henry. She was daughter to Charles the Bad, monarch of the Basque kingdom of Navarre, and it was Navarrese ambassadors who brokered what was to be a very controversial marriage between the two. The negotiations had of necessity been conducted in secret. Relations between England and France had at this point deteriorated too far for a marriage of this kind to have had any significant beneficial impact, and rather it seems that Henry, who simultaneously arranged political marriages for his two daughters, Blanche and Philippa, hoped to forge family ties across Europe that would legitimise his kingship.

The marriage was not easily made. Henry was Joan's third cousin twice over and marriages with this degree of consanguinity required a papal dispensation. This was complicated by the continuing schism, under which the French recognised the Avignon pontiff, Benedict XIII, while England recognised the Roman pope, Boniface IX. Joan eventually obtained permission from Pope Benedict and the two were married by proxy at Eltham on April 2nd 1402. Joan was not to join her husband until the following year and even her passage to England was eventful. She embarked at Camaret, south of Brest, on January 13th 1403, with the intention of landing at Southampton. Strong, adverse winds forced a change of plan and, after a stormy, five-day passage, she was obliged to land at Falmouth – nearly two hundred miles further from London than had been intended. The new queen's arrival, on an easterly gale in January, must have been an extremely cold and miserable affair.

Her political welcome was scarcely any warmer. Henry's subjects, far from seeing the marriage as constructive diplomacy, were astonished to see him marrying a duchess from the enemy camp, whilst the French were outraged at her marriage to the man who had usurped Richard and thereby denied the throne of England to a French princess. Far from pacifying the Bretons, the marriage resulted in intensified hostility and increased attacks on English interests.

In the spring of 1403, Hawley received an official commission to man certain of his ships and barges with two hundred men and go to sea against the king's enemies – presumably a reference to increasing breaches of the truce by Bretons – and, in the months that followed, he was increasingly treated as if he held some official rank. As late as the middle of 1403, it seems that neither government wished to acknowledge the fact which would have been obvious to anyone who had reason to cross the sea – that England and France had been at war for some time. The fact was, however, becoming increasingly difficult to ignore, as the pitched battles which were being fought on an increasingly large scale at sea started to spill over in to coastal areas on both sides of the Channel.

The accounts of the chroniclers of the time were generally based on hearsay evidence which was subject to exaggeration and self-serving interpretation and must be treated with caution[*], but French sources speak of the defeat of a large force of English pirates off St Mathieu in July 1403, in which a large number of English vessels and prisoners were taken and no small number of 'soldiers' thrown into the sea. It was the arrival of the conflict on home soil, however, which finally produced an official response from Henry. On August 9th that year, a Breton force, under William du Châtel, Lord of Chateauneuf in Brittany, landed near Plymouth and attacked it from the rear, burning, pillaging and extracting ransom without meeting any significant resistance. On August 26th the Council issued:

> *"Commission to the Mayor,[†] John Haule, John Corp and Edmund Arnold in Dertemuth to make war on the men of Brittany who have broken the late truces of Leulyngham made between the King and the French"*[82]

Even here, Henry was trying to ward off a full-scale war by drawing a clear distinction between the dukedom of Brittany and the kingdom of France, which could often, for diplomatic purposes, be regarded as separate political entities. If the Dartmouth privateers understood, or were interested in, the distinction, however, it made no practical difference to them. They were at war again.

There has been some debate as to how much control Henry was able to exert over the activities of the privateers where vessels from countries other than France were concerned. Certainly there was a marked increase in claims against Hawley and the others in respect of seizures in the latter part of 1403 and into 1404, from shipowners and merchants of Spain, Lombardy, Florence, Castile and Piedmont. This may suggest that, following the commission of August 1403, the Dartmouth men had simply plundered anything that moved in the Channel indiscriminately. It is much more likely, however, that these claims were just the tip of the iceberg and reflected the usual practice of stopping and searching any ship which might be suspected of carrying enemy goods – that is to say virtually any ship – and confiscating the goods where there was any reason or excuse to be suspicious. It seems likely that, for every neutral vessel thus intercepted, several French ships were attacked. If so, it indicates that the number of legitimate privateering attacks, on the vessels of France and her allies, increased dramatically in the months over which the two nations plunged

---

[*] *The chroniclers of the fourteenth century were, for the most part, clergymen, and the purpose of their writings was moralistic rather than historical. As such, they were sometimes inclined to subjugate factual accuracy to a desire to extract a moral from the story.*

[†] *There is no record of who held the office in 1403*

towards formally declared war. This picture is consistent with the nature of known official commissions and organised campaigns and suggests that official and unofficial raids on shipping by both sides proceeded in parallel.[83]

It is clear that the ports of south-west England were on a full war footing in late 1403. In January 1404, the masters of eleven ships of Southampton and other ports which had been held for so long at Dartmouth under arrest for the king's service that they had run out of victuals and other supplies and had been obliged to return to Southampton for replenishment, were officially pardoned for doing so.[84] They were not, it seems, simply evading royal service in the hope of more gainful action but had taken on supplies and were awaiting orders by the Isle of Wight. The fact that they had been unable to re-supply at Dartmouth suggests that the town was at this point at the centre of a mass naval mobilisation and that the local infrastructure was simply unable to cope with the demands of the ships which crowded in.

It has often been suggested that the fighting which erupted in the latter part of 1403 was the result of an escalation of the long-running feud between the men of Dartmouth and their Breton counterparts and this no doubt fuelled passions on both sides, but the fighting can also be seen as an extension of a broader conflict which, although undeclared, had been gathering momentum for three years and more. Reprisals there certainly were, but these were highly organised and, as evidenced by the August 1403 commission, officially sanctioned. Whether, in its earlier stages, it had been a 'pirate war' or not, it was certainly much more than that by the autumn of 1403.

In October 1403, Hawley and Thomas Norton of Bristol were serving as 'admirals' of the fleets of Bristol, Plymouth and Dartmouth and are known to have been at sea, complying with the August commission to take the fight to the Bretons. This they did in their characteristic style and, as was their custom, they routinely seized the cargos of any foreign vessels which had not been granted clear and watertight protection. In the course of this expedition they made routine captures of a number of Castilian vessels. On October 18th they seized a barge called *Seint Julien* and took her to 'Beleista' [Belle Île?] in Brittany, where they unloaded 2,036 bars of iron before scuttling her. On the same day, they took two other Castilian vessels – the *Seint Johan* with her cargo of 1,382 iron bars and thirty quintals* of rosin and the *Seynt Piere*, carrying a similar cargo – and sent them as prizes to their home ports.[85] On October 27th they took another Castilian ship, the *Seint Nicholl*, laden with wheat, peas and cloth.[86] This is one of the few occasions where we see clear evidence of Hawley at sea and acting out his legendary role as privateer admiral. The time and care dedicated to the taking of prizes indicates that, even in this time of national emergency and undeclared war, and when they had clear official sanction to seek out and destroy the enemy, Hawley and Norton were unable to resist the temptation of easy plunder. In all, seven Castilian vessels were taken in this manner and the spoils of this expedition were to cause Hawley some trouble later.

---

* *About 1½ tons.*

The more specific, official response to du Châtel's attack on Plymouth in August was immediate and savage. On this occasion, the king's orders passed to William Wilford, the MP for Exeter and a man from a similar background to Hawley, to bring together the fleets from Dartmouth, Bristol and Plymouth and take the fight back to Brittany. Wilford's substantial force, which probably included ships owned by Hawley, sailed straight for the familiar waters off Brest and proceeded to wreak havoc among the shipping along the coast. They immediately captured six foreign cargo vessels and took another four the following day, before heading south to Belle Île, where they seized an entire wine fleet, of thirty or forty ships of La Rochelle, carrying off about a thousand tuns of wine. They then returned northwards, landing on the promontory of Penmarch, and marched eighteen miles inland, plundering, reportedly with great brutality, as they went. The 'barbican' outpost of Brest had been relinquished by Richard II in 1397 and it was to this area that they finally returned, burning "*Ste Matthieu*' (presumably Le Conquet) and offering battle to an army near Brest – which offer was declined – before returning home with the spoils.

Wilford's expedition had amounted to a significant escalation of the conflict and an affront to the chivalric class of Brittany. William du Châtel asked permission of the princes of France, who were ruling in a collective regency because of the king's insanity, to mount a substantial expedition in response. Then, together with the lords of Chateaubriand and de Jaille, he assembled a fleet which the chronicle of the Monk of St Denys put at three hundred ships, embarking two thousand knights and esquires, men-at-arms and crossbowmen, with the intention of making a retaliatory strike at Dartmouth.

Even allowing for the exaggeration often seen in the French chronicles of the time, this was a very substantial force, but the habitually uncoordinated nature of the French military command structure at the time was soon to render it less threatening than it might have been. The day after they sailed, they encountered some Spanish vessels carrying wine which, the Franco-Spanish alliance notwithstanding, they seized and, allegedly, drank. This gave rise to a quarrel among the commanders and the formation split, the forces under Chateaubriand proceeding independently. Contemporary accounts of what happened when du Châtel and de Jaille's troops arrived in Devon are confusing and often contradictory, but Russell[87] suggests that the *Chronique de St Denys* offers the most accurate and detailed account. Hawley was subsequently to refer to the battle which ensued as the '*scomfiture at Blakpolle*', which identifies the location quite closely, and the Monk gives a dramatic insight into the psyche of the Breton Lords. The nature of the battle, however, can perhaps best be inferred with reference to the fragmentary evidence gleaned from all contemporary and near-contemporary accounts, the nature of the opposing forces and the constraints which the topography imposed on the tactics.

It was undoubtedly a depleted Breton force which landed in April 1404, but just how depleted is not known. It is said to have lacked the contingent of (usually Genoese, mercenary) crossbowmen which normally preceded French cavalry attacks and the total numbers are also unknown. It was also, perhaps crucially, operating under at least two commanders.

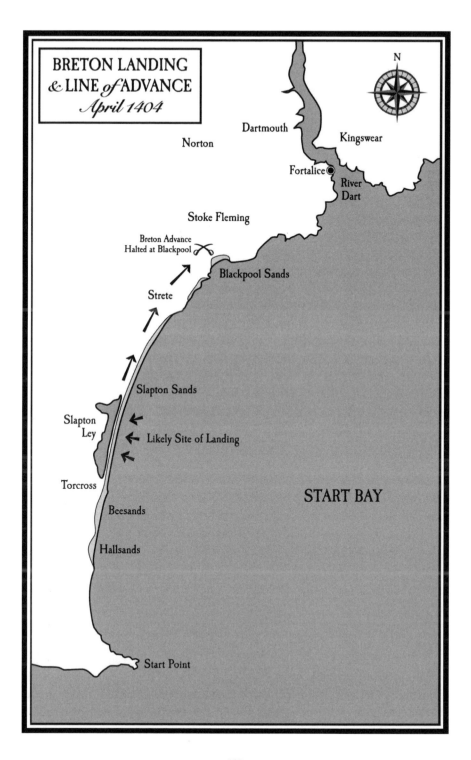

BRETON LANDING
& LINE of ADVANCE
April 1404

N

Dartmouth

Kingswear

Norton

Fortalice

River
Dart

Stoke Fleming

Breton Advance
Halted at Blackpool

Blackpool Sands

Strete

Slapton Sands

Slapton
Ley

Likely Site of Landing

Torcross

START BAY

Beesands

Hallsands

Start Point

Hawley is credited with having played a major part in organising the defences. His role in the battle is unknown and it is generally assumed that he remained in Dartmouth, overseeing the defences surrounding the fortalice. If so, he would not have been hemmed in at the fortalice and, the rocky stretch of the coastline between the mouth of the Dart and Blackpool being practically impregnable, he could have ridden the three miles between there and the scene of the unfolding battle, across the unenclosed fields of the parish of Stoke Fleming, in less than an hour, without fear of encountering enemy troops landing there. It is unlikely that a man of his advanced age would have engaged in hand-to-hand fighting in any event but he could have played a significant part in commanding the forces which were drawn up in defence. There is, however, no evidence that he was present at Blackpool and it might reasonably be inferred from the wording of his subsequent letter to the king that he was not.

Nor is the nature of the defending force exactly known, but the suggestion in the *Chronique* that it consisted of six thousand men must be a considerable exaggeration, bearing in mind that the standing army of the whole of England at the time was of the order of ten thousand. It was certainly an irregular peasant and yeoman army but, given the high level of preparedness and the predominantly military and paranaval nature of the temporarily swollen population of Dartmouth, it would not have been lacking in experienced fighters and may have been stiffened by some seasoned professionals.

The local topography had a critical influence on what happened at the Battle of Blackpool. Whereas Wilford's troops landing at Penmarch had doubtless done so on the firm, gently shelving white sands of the beach at la Torche, du Châtel, faced with the ironclad coastline which defends the immediate vicinity of Dartmouth, had the more difficult task of disembarking his cavalry and foot soldiers with their horses and equipment on one of the steep, pebble beaches to the south-west of the town, either at Blackpool or Slapton. Some accounts imply that the Bretons landed on Blackpool beach in small numbers, perhaps no more than two hundred, and proceeded to battle without waiting for the main body of their force, including the crossbowmen, to land. This seems highly unlikely, as the half-mile, crescent beach at Blackpool is more prone to heavy surf than the near-straight three miles of Slapton and is overlooked by an easily defended hill, which would have rendered the disembarking troops extremely vulnerable to the attentions of the archers. It would simply have been an unlikely choice. Slapton is the more likely location of the landing because, for most of its length, the beach there is backed by a freshwater lake and marshland, giving no natural advantage to the defenders. If, as Russell suggests and as seems most likely, du Châtel landed at Slapton, with the intention of attacking Dartmouth from the rear, he would have had to take his soldiers up the moderate ascent to Strete and then across the deep valley which opens to the sea at Blackpool, before crossing three miles or so of undulating farmland.

It was at Blackpool that the local defenders had chosen to fight – and with good reason. The valley is narrow and steep-sided, and any flanking force moving through it would have been vulnerable to attack from the valley sides, whilst the western side is impassably steep for most of its length. Only at the southern end, where it opens onto the wide pebble beach, does the slope moderate somewhat and it was probably here, on April 15th, as du Châtel's men descended the steep western slope and tried to cross the valley bottom, that the battle was joined. A substantial stream flows down the valley and the defenders are said in the French chronicles to have dug a defensive water-filled ditch, leaving only an easily defended 'causeway'. An observer unfamiliar with the location may have been unable to distinguish between a causeway and a temporary dam and it is perhaps more likely that the stream had been dammed for the width of the valley bottom, flooding most of the already-limited flat ground, as an impediment to the attackers.

The defenders had arrayed themselves on the hill leading up to Stoke Fleming, probably with woodland to their rear. There it can safely be assumed that they adopted some version of the classic, defensive configuration used by the English in every battle with the French since Crécy and it is likely, as in the earlier fights and eleven years later at Agincourt, that it was the longbow which was the decisive weapon. It was the perfect place for a defensive battle in the English style. A complete lack of clear, flat ground would have hampered any opposing cavalry and would have made it impossible for du Châtel to concentrate large numbers of his troops in any defensible formation. The marshy and likely flooded valley bottom would have made movement extremely difficult for armoured knights and the bottleneck rendered them vulnerable to the volleys from the bowmen – their light, flight arrows from two hundred yards and more, and the heavier, bodkin-tipped shafts at closer quarters. Without his crossbowmen, du Châtel would have had no answer to the yeoman archers.

The Monk of St Denys reports that, confronted with this defensive force, du Châtel advised caution but that de Jaille, by implying that he was guilty of cowardice, goaded him into a reckless attack. Du Châtel is reported to have said:

"God forbid that the heart of a Breton should know so disgraceful a sentiment! Convinced as I am that we march to death rather than to victory, I will take the chance of a battle; let the die be cast, for I vow to God I will not this day be put to ransom".[88]

With that, the chronicle states that he and his followers threw themselves on the enemy and killed fifteen hundred of them before being themselves slain. The account goes on to say that William du Châtel, 'the flower of chivalry', fell mortally wounded and expired as his captors, having carried him to the town, dressed his wounds. The other Breton division, presumably under de Jaille, then attempted to cross the water-filled ditch, misjudging its depth, and many drowned, dragged down by the weight of their armour. Any that made the eastern bank were killed or taken prisoner.

This reads as a romanticised account and it seems highly unlikely that du Châtel's attack against a defending host which he evidently found daunting could have inflicted so many casualties; this claim being perhaps an attempt to put a brave face on a military disaster. It also, perhaps, reflects the disdain with which the French aristocracy at this time treated their social inferiors. French knights routinely rode down their own foot soldiers and crossbowmen in their attacks[*] and, in this light, it is easy to see how du Châtel, when confronted with an irregular peasant and yeoman army, however numerically superior, may readily have been goaded into an impetuous attack.

One account suggests that the defenders, seeing that the enemy numbered no more than two hundred or so, were emboldened to move down to the valley bottom to attack them. It seems extremely unlikely that, having mounted such a substantial expedition, the French would have deliberately landed so small a number and, if true, suggests that they suffered some tactical dislocation, possibly due to the restrictive nature of the terrain or, more likely, other defensive action. A clue to the resolution of this puzzle might be found in Robert Fabyan's 'Concordaunce of Hystoryes', published after his death in 1516, which offers another version of the battle, describing it as a sea fight. This is not necessarily inconsistent with other accounts and the addition of a naval dimension may explain the failure of du Châtel to deploy the bulk of his troops. Fabyan offers that the French chroniclers:

> "...excuseth this scomfiture of Frenchmen and saith that, by treason of a Gascone named Peryn or Perot de Languyle, which shewed unto the said Lord Castyle that he had espied certain English ships in a creek lightly without resistance to be taken, caused the said lord to make sail towards the said town of Dartmouth, where, after he had continued a certain time his course, he espied the whole fleet of Englishmen, which made towards him and so at the said Blackpool encountered and fought, and lastly escaped the danger of his enemies, as testified the said French chronicle, but not unhurt, for he was so wounded in the fight that he died shortly after."[89]

This clearly implies that du Châtel died in a sea fight, which is inconsistent with the more credible St Denys claim that he died of his wounds while a prisoner – and with the subsequent petition from his brother to the mayor of Dartmouth for the release of his body. As such, this account, which was written years after the event, should be treated with caution but the rather detailed description suggests that there was a significant naval element in the Battle of Blackpool. If the St Denys suggestion that the fleet numbered three hundred sail is discounted to a more reasonable number and if, as seems to have been the case, it was further depleted before it arrived, it is

---

[*] *Genoese crossbowmen, retreating because they had shot all their bolts, were, for example, ridden down by the advancing French cavalry at Crécy.*

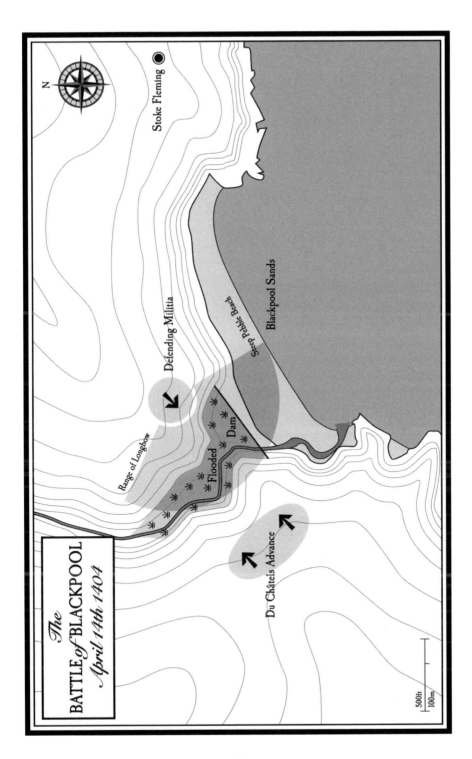

The
BATTLE of BLACKPOOL
April 14th 1404

Stoke Fleming

Defending Militia

Blackpool Sands

Steep Pebble Beach

Range of Longbow

Dam

Flooded

Du Châtels Advance

500ft
100m

unlikely that Hawley and the other local defenders would have been intimidated into mounting a purely land-based defence. If the defenders were expecting the arrival of a significant force which included cavalry, and had sufficient ships available to respond, it would have made sense for them to attack the Breton ships before they landed the troops, when the horses and other related equipment would have been a liability to the attackers and not the significant asset which they would become if they were allowed to disembark. The *Chronique* implies that du Châtel himself dismounted to lead the attack at Blackpool and that he was followed by the others. This implies that the Bretons had been able to land some cavalry but if, as is likely, their landing was opposed, it was probably only a limited force, and one without crossbowmen, that actually fought ashore at Blackpool, the remainder being repulsed or destroyed at sea.

Given the evidence of a substantial paranaval force having been present in Dartmouth in early 1404, with the express purpose of protecting against exactly this kind of attack, it seems unlikely that the Westcountrymen, who had by now been fighting the French at sea across three generations, would have failed to do so in the face of an imminent threat to their homes. Some of the detail of Fabyan's description of the battle, which also states that many ships were taken in the action, does not fit easily with other accounts and may be unreliable in some respects, but its general thrust must be taken seriously and it is almost inconceivable that Hawley, who is generally credited with having played a substantial role in organising the land defences, would have entirely eschewed his accustomed role as an impresario of sea fights when everything that he held dear was imperilled. In all, it seems that a robust naval defence probably was deployed, raising the question as to why no contemporary records of either the naval aspect of the battle, or of Hawley's specific role in it, have survived.

The answer to this may lie in contemporary attitudes to the celebrated land battle, and in what was considered to be remarkable about it at the time. The Battle of Blackpool ended in the manner typical of such encounters in the late Middle Ages with the merciless slaughter of the low-ranking wounded and captives (whose cries for mercy were said to have been interpreted by the monoglot peasantry as shouts of defiance and duly ignored) and the ransoming of the higher ranks. Subsequent English accounts put the French death toll at about five hundred and make no mention of English casualties. Legend has it that even the local women helped to secure the prisoners, having belaboured the French troops with their slingshots and, while improbable*, there may be some grain of truth in the legend. In any event, the persistence of the story indicates how, to a highly class-conscious society, the one-sided slaughter of regular soldiers and, in particular, of knights, by a plebeian militia was quite sensational.

---

* *Russell suggests that this is an apocryphal borrowing from a battle at Portland, the inhabitants of which had a tradition of defensive stone-throwing which earned it the name "Isle of Slingers"*

The peasant army had produced a haul of three lords and twenty knights for ransom, a result which the French chroniclers no doubt found difficult to stomach. One remarked that *"The crows have pecked the eagles"*, while the astonishment of the ruling classes of England was clearly expressed when the king ordered a *Te Deum* to be sung in thanksgiving in Westminster Abbey. By comparison with this, a conventional sea battle, prosecuted by paranaval forces which had been busily engaged in just such fighting for the past four years, would have been literally unremarkable and, if the Battle of Blackpool was indeed fought on the water as well as the land, this aspect may therefore have gone largely unreported. If there was a significant naval element to the engagement, it also, of course, raises the possibility that our old privateer was not coordinating land defences on the day but was at sea – playing the part of an admiral rather than that of a general. He had commanded his own ships during the excursion with Norton six months earlier and there is no reason to believe that he was unable or disinclined to do so now.

The suggestion of one chronicler that du Châtel's brother returned a month later and razed Dartmouth in revenge seems fanciful; there is no record of any such attack on the English side and it is known that, three months after the battle, John Hawley was sitting at home in Dartmouth, writing to the king about the ransom of the captives. The crisis, it seems, had passed.

On April 20th , Henry commissioned one Nicholas Aldewiche, esquire, to *"... bring five, six or seven of the more valid and sufficient of the King's enemies lately captured near Dertemuth to the King's presence to enquire of them."*[90] A commission to the Sheriff of Devon, dated five days later, was more specific, requiring delivery of:

> *"...Bertram de Guytyn chivaler, John Gaudyn chivaler, Oliver Arell chivaler, Tange de Chastelle, Henry de Chastelle and a certain Welsh esquire*, captured by the King's lieges, that the King may have colloquy with them and learn the secrets of his enemies."*[91]

Hawley had purchased half-shares[†] in the ransoms of two of the above-named and, while he released Oliver Arell into the custody of the sergeant at arms promptly, he had for some reason failed to hand over the more valuable *"Chastelle"* [Tange du Châtel – brother of William]. The consequent summons to account occasioned the only surviving letter from Hawley. In formally oleaginous Norman French, to Henry IV – whose first language was French – Hawley or, more likely, an amanuensis[‡] writes:

---

[*] *Evidence of some involvement of Welsh rebels in the Breton expedition*

[†] *The word moiety denotes a half share, although it may have been used more loosely by Hawley in this instance to denote a complete purchase.*

[‡] *I am indebted to Dr. Jenny Stratford of the Institute of Historical Research, the University of London, who has viewed the document and confirms that it is almost certainly the work of a professional scribe, writing in an early secretarial hand with anglicana features.*

The only surviving letter from John Hawley was penned in 1404, by a scribe, in Norman French, to Henry IV, whose first language was French.

"Humbly I recommend myself to your majesty. May it please your Majesty to know that I have received your gracious letter making mention that I ought to appear in person before your Majesty on the Monday next after the feast of St. Margaret*, in whatever place you might happen to be. May it please your Majesty to hold me excused for that I cannot come myself in person before your Majesty. Know that I have been suffering from so severe a disorder in one of my legs for more than a month that I cannot ride and am not well able to walk. And if it please your Majesty, touching the prisoner Oliver Avelle, a Breton, Richard Keyne came to me and offered to sell the moiety in the said prisoner in 'le scomfiture à Blakpolle' the which prisoner, your Majesty, I have sent to Your Majesty's presence. And if it please your Majesty, know that I have and have purchased of Anthony John the moiety in Tange Castelle, brother to the

---

* *The feast of St Margaret appears as July 20ᵗʰ in Anglo-Saxon calendars although it was subsequently moved to June 19ᵗʰ until the Reformation, when it became June 10ᵗʰ, eventually moving to November 16ᵗʰ in 1972. Assuming that Hawley's syntax is appropriate to the time of writing, the king was probably using the Anglo-Saxon date, implying an order to attend him on Monday July 21ˢᵗ 1404. If so, this letter would barely have reached its royal addressee before Hawley's absence was noted.*

Detail of the Hawley letter – The reference to the Battle of Blackpool as 'le scomfiture à Blakpolle' can be discerned in the highlighted text.
Courtesy of the British Library

> *Lord of Castelle, prisoner, the which Tange is at your Majesty's disposal, that it may please your Majesty to ordain for me and for no other. For the said Anthony John was at his taking before the jurors of Blakpolle and had a share of the booty with Stephen Modbury. And your Majesty may Almighty God grant to you good life and long and increase you in joys and honours before all other Lords living in the world.*
>
> *At Dartmouth, the 14th day of July*
> *Your poor liege, if it please your high lordship*
>
> *Johan Hawley de Dertemouthe"[92]*

Hawley's scribe may have provided the obligatory, forelock-tugging verbiage but it must have been Hawley himself who provided the burden of the message; and the letter is almost impudent in its content. Having excused himself from the summons to the king's presence, Hawley concedes custody of du Châtel, while staking his claim to the ransom proceeds and reminding the sovereign of the undertaking in the commission to Aldwiche that "...*each of the King's lieges shall have his profit from his prisoners*"[93].

The reference to the severe disorder in one of his legs is the only clue available to us regarding his physical condition. He was by now an old man and, although this 'disorder' may have been the result of an accident – a fall from a horse perhaps – he was more likely suffering from some chronic disease. As a wealthy man of his time, he probably consumed large amounts of wine and red meat, making him particularly susceptible to gout. An attack of a month or more suggests chronic, rather than acute, gout, but it is also possible that he was being gradually crippled by some form of arthritis. In either event, no effective medical treatment would have been available to him and, unless his claim of physical disability was merely an excuse for not attending the king, the impression given is of a man who, while of undiminished mental energy, was in the early stages of an irreversible and untreatable physical decline. He was probably condemned to suffering chronic pain for the rest of his life.

After the battle of Blackpool, the French made no further direct assaults on Dartmouth and the focus of the action moved eastwards. On March 18th 1406, Hawley was the first named in a commission to no fewer than twenty-four local men to *"... survey all defects in the town and port of Dertemuth and fortify the town..."*[4], but these were routine precautionary measures and, in his role as valiant defender of the town and the realm, the Battle of Blackpool had been his glorious swansong. The Hawley family business, however, had a momentum of its own, and he was to continue to be cited as defendant in claims relating to privateering until the last months of his life.

If the privateering ventures of Hawley and the other Dartmouth oligarchs had a momentum all their own, so, it seems, did the bureaucracy of international diplomacy and the courts which adjudicated on the issues raised by their activities. It is perhaps ironic that, in the spring of 1404, while John Hawley was supervising preparations for a pitched battle on behalf of the king, demands were being issued in the name of that same sovereign that he should make restitution to the Castilian merchants whose ships and goods he and Thomas Norton had seized during the previous October. In May 1403, Henry had informed the mayor and burgesses of Dartmouth that a treaty of friendship was pending between England and Castile and that the town's privateers should, accordingly, exercise restraint. During the negotiation of this treaty, Henry had granted safe passage to all Castilian ships for a limited period, ending on September 29th of that year. Norton and Hawley therefore had legal justification for their actions in October, but diplomatic considerations trumped such legal niceties and Henry issued the orders for restitution.

Compliance with this order in respect of one ship was, however, to prove problematical. Garsius Piers, the master of the *Seint Johan,* which had been among the seven Castilians captured in October, sought and was granted restitution and the Bristol men soon gave up the ship and part of her cargo. The bulk of the cargo and much of the ship's gear, however, was sitting on Hawley's hoe in Dartmouth. The king on January 16th ordered both the elder and younger John Hawleys to hand over the goods or to appear in person at Westminster by February 9th if they wished to argue the point. It is perhaps understandable, in the circumstances, that the man overseeing the preparation of Dartmouth for an imminent attack declined this offer to treat, but neither, it seems, did he comply with the restitution order in full. Hawley's letter to the king in July can thus be seen as making an excuse for a second failure to comply with a royal summons, and we may detect in its tone a stubbornness born of a belief that, in his various strategic roles, he was too important to be subjected to this kind of demand at this particular time. He was, at any rate, slow to comply with orders. Henry was seen to complain in March 1404 that 'certain of his lieges' were withholding the goods against his orders and instructed that they be arrested if they did not make restitution.[95] There are no further references to the case in the Patent Rolls and so Hawley and the rest presumably complied eventually.

One scholar who has made a particular study of the relations between Hawley and Henry IV suggests that the king was by now becoming increasingly exasperated with the antics of his Westcountry mariner subjects in general and with Hawley in particular[96] and this would have certainly been an understandable sentiment. Henry was by now, however, extremely ill* and still had more to occupy his mind than the excesses of Hawley and his like, and so it seems unlikely that he was behind the change in the official attitude towards the privateers that became apparent in 1406. It does appear that someone in Henry's court was convinced that barely controlled privateering was not a suitable mechanism for the defence of the seas in the longer run, and it is possible that the nineteen year-old Prince Henry, the future Henry V, was beginning to involve himself in naval affairs – a subject in which he was in future to exhibit a particular interest, and for which he had a considerable talent.

The Long Parliament of March 1406 discussed a plan under which naval defences would continue to be in the hands of merchants and shipowners but they would operate under parliamentary ordinance and would be funded out of customs revenues. The arrangement finally approved was:

> *"...that the merchants of the kingdom of England shall be responsible for the guarding of the sea from 1 May next until the following feast of Michaelmas, and from the same feast of Michaelmas for one whole year until the next feast of Michaelmas: and that from the said 1 May until 1 November next they shall have 2,000 fighting men adequately equipped for war, in addition to a satisfactory and sufficient number of mariners for the manning of the ships in time of war; and from the said 1 November until the following 1 May, 1,000 fighting men suitably arrayed; and from the same 1 May until the following feast of St Michael, 2,000 fighting men, in addition to a satisfactory and sufficient number of mariners, as above; and sometimes more fighting men, as needs be."* [97]

---

* *The king's ailments and their symptoms were a closely guarded secret and it is impossible to diagnose what was wrong with him. He had been in poor health, at least intermittently, for several years.*

The shipowners thus agreed to provide ships to embark specified numbers of fighting men for a period of sixteen months from May that year and, in return, would receive the proceeds of a quarter of the subsidy on wool, hides and wool fells and a quarter of the customs revenues from other types of merchandise. In addition, the mariners were to be entitled to their traditional prizes, although the Crown retained a right of first refusal on high-ranking captives, in return for suitable rewards. Similar arrangements had been put in place ahead of the siege of Calais, but this seems to have been more an attempt to regularise access to ships and to gain some degree of control over their owners' activities than a response to a particular emergency or military need. The purpose of the arrangement was specifically 'the guard of the sea', which implies that it amounted to a contract for the hire of a mercenary navy for a fixed period. It is clear that the two appointed admirals – Nicholas Blackburn for the north and Richard Clitheroe for the south and west – did start to implement the scheme but it was not to last. In the very last act of the Long Parliament, just six months later, the merchants were released from their responsibilities, and arrangements made for reimbursing them for expenses incurred.

It is not known exactly why this initiative failed but it seems most likely that the Crown simply decided that it could not afford it. Certainly the king was under extreme financial pressure as the parliament sat into the exceptionally hot summer of 1406 and he was attempting, by mid-September, to divert into the exchequer the revenues which had been allocated to the merchants for the defence of the seas. The fiscal basis for the scheme was further undermined when, in response to another petition, the additional twelve pence to be levied on aliens in respect of tonnage and poundage was abolished. It is anyway likely that those among the shipowners who were established privateers found the economics of operating under centralised control unattractive, even if the scheme underwrote their basic expenses. They, after all, knew better than anyone how to profit from fighting the king's enemies and anyone else who might appear to be in their service.

In any event, the privateers went back to business as usual and the nature of the claims lodged against them during this period suggests that they did so more aggressively and indiscriminately than ever. The stiffening of the official mood, however, was soon to have severe implications for Hawley, culminating in his last, dramatic appearance in the official record.

At some time in 1406 a carrack of Barcelona, carrying an unusually valuable cargo of spices, wines and other goods went ashore in a storm on the Hampshire coast. The ship was formally under the protection of letters of safe conduct but this did not prevent wreckers, in barges of Kent, Sussex and Devon, from assaulting the crew, looting the cargo and destroying the ship. Hawley's men must have been involved in this incident, although he is not named in

Cold comfort – the elderly Hawley spent the Christmas of 1406 in the Tower of London.

Engraving from 'The Antiquities of England and Wales 1783'

any of the relevant commissions and, but for the very high value of the cargo seized, it may have passed as just one of the many claims which had been lodged against him, almost routinely, over his long career. This time, however, it was different and, on December 15th 1406, the Constable of the Tower of London was ordered to receive him and to keep him in safe custody in the Tower until further notice.[98]

It is ironic that, after a lifetime of straight-arming the judicial system, and having won social rank, personal prestige and patriotic glory in no small measure, the old privateer should suddenly find himself incarcerated in the Tower for an incident in which he was certainly not directly involved and in which even his indirect involvement was as one of many. In any event, his luck, or perhaps just official patience, had run out and he had been chosen as a hostage against the return of the Spanish cargo. He was released on February 4th, having undertaken, under pain of a fine of £10,000, not to leave the king's court without leave of the king or Council and to make full restitution of any property of merchants of Barcelona, taken by his servants at sea, which came into his hands. Three Cornishmen, including Sir John Arundell of Lanherne, the former husband of Margaret Tresilian, and two men of Devon stood surety for him to the tune of £3,000 and the order against Hawley was cancelled by the Chancellor on February 5th 1407 because its terms had been observed.

While the sixty-six year-old Hawley was awaiting His Majesty's pleasure in the Tower, Henry IV, who was twenty-seven years his junior, spent the Christmas of 1406 at Eltham Palace with his queen. The king was sick, impecunious and despondent and, although he survived until March 1413, his severe illness rendered him increasingly immobile and impinged on his ability to govern. The decision to imprison Hawley was almost certainly taken by someone else. The Tower was always a place for important prisoners and we have no reason to believe that Hawley's incarceration would have been anything other than humane, resembling perhaps a rather Spartan house arrest, but the winters of the early fifteenth century were extremely cold and the four-hundred-mile round-trip on horseback from Dartmouth, in the depths of winter, must have been painful for an old, tired and probably sick man. He was to survive this and the famously severe winter of 1407, but it is likely that his physical decline was by now faster than that of his king and there is no further sighting of him in action after his return from imprisonment.

In the last year of his life, the elder John Hawley, even if he was personally incapacitated and largely inactive, had become an almost legendary figure and was still treated by the government as if he were the admiral of the Dartmouth privateers, who were now running out of control. In 1408, John Arundell, who had stood surety for him in February of the previous year, and his friend John Corp, were among those commissioned by the Crown to arrest him and bring him before the Council, together with some twenty-five other privateers from southern and western ports, ten of whom were operating out of Dartmouth, to answer charges in connection with the capture at sea of ten Breton ships, which were by now protected by treaty. He was perhaps no longer physically able to make the arduous journey to Westminster and there is, at any rate, no record of his having answered his accusers on this occasion.

John Hawley died in Dartmouth on December 30th 1408, still contesting claims for substantial sums from neutral merchants whose cargoes his men had seized, and was buried in modest splendour in the chancel of the Trinity Church, of which he had been a founding benefactor. He was a privateer – and obstinate – to the last.

Chapter Six:

The Man, his Son and the Hawley Legend

John the Younger

The elder John Hawley had been a Dartmouth man from first to last. Dartmouth had been his power base, almost his fiefdom, and he never lived anywhere else. It is not known how often, or for how long, he visited his Cornish estates, but the extent of his recorded movements in Dartmouth, in Westminster and at sea, suggests that he was little more than an absentee landlord there.

The Dartmouth loyalties of John Hawley the younger were not so exclusive. As his father's only child, he inherited the shipping interests, as well as the Cornish estates, and he was certainly an active privateer in his father's mould. The elder Hawley and Thomas Asshenden were of the generation of Dartmouth privateer merchants that developed the model of paranaval service to the Crown and, with the ground rules thus laid down, the younger Hawley was drawn into various official roles within this system at a relatively early age. He certainly spent part of his life in London, at the court of Richard II, and there is a probable reference to him in November 1400, as a "king's servant" to whom, with two others, are granted "...*monies pertaining to the King for the escape of eight prisoners...from the prison of Northampton on 18 November last*"[99], which suggests that he acted in some general, administrative capacity at that time. He is sometimes referred to as John Hawley of Dartmouth and Trematon* and acted as a justice of the peace in Cornwall later in his life.

It was primarily as a Dartmouth privateer, however, that the younger John was known, and he followed in his father's footsteps sufficiently closely in this regard that historians have sometimes struggled to distinguish between references to

---

Just to the west of Saltash.

the two of them. His favour at court seems to have survived the regime change of 1399 and, in 1401, he was appointed to the important post of controller of customs revenues collected in the port of London. He returned to Dartmouth from London in 1402, when he was appointed as feodary* and escheator in the Duchy of Cornwall. He appeared occasionally at the Court of Chancery in this connection but, in the early 1400s, with the phoney war at sea intensifying and Dartmouth under threat, he joined his father in dedicating most of his energies to maritime affairs.

It might be suggested that, in his dealings with officialdom, the younger Hawley picked up where the elder left off but he had, in fact, even before the elder John's death, adopted his father's style of robust, litigious give and take – always with an eye to the changing political and diplomatic situation. There was to be a seamless continuity in the Hawley family's turbulent relationship with authority. The father and son were first named together in an order to make restitution in November 1403, against a claim by Piedmontese merchants, among whom one Richard Garner, who was resident in London, was notable for having fallen foul of Hawley's men on at least two previous occasions.[100] The Hawleys clearly had more pressing matters to attend to as the Breton invasion loomed and, predictably, the Italians were still pursuing the case in the following year.

In September 1404, the king issued a commission from Tutbury Castle to the sheriff of Devon to enforce restitution, by the 'octaves of Michaelmas' [October 6th] to one John Disco of *"Pampilion"* [Pamplona] of twenty-two tuns of oil, which had been captured at sea by *"certain people"* of Bristol, Dartmouth and Plymouth *"under penalty of £100".*[101] The oil in question, almost certainly part of the spoils of the Hawley-Norton cruise of 1403, had been taken to Dartmouth, by assent of the whole privateer fleet, and had been put under the custody of, among others, both the elder and younger Hawleys. Disco, having failed to convince the captors that the oil was his, had received certification from the king of Navarre as to his ownership and we may assume that, at that point, Henry was under some diplomatic pressure from his brother-in-law to see that the goods were returned or compensation rendered. The response from Dartmouth had nonetheless been tardy, the Hawleys and the other respondents having already failed to respond to *"divers writs"* from the king, and the September commission was a reminder. It was, however, a reminder which was not heeded, and it was necessary to issue a further commission in December, ordering compliance by *"the morrow of St Mathias the Apostle"*†, turning up the heat with a threat of an increased fine of £200.

---

* An officer of the Court of Wards

† As with many saints' days, this changed over the centuries and varies between denominations of the church but, in this case, it probably refers to February 24th.

Exactly how the case of John Disco's oil was resolved is unclear but it had been resolved and the younger Hawley was once again in good standing in October 1406, when *"...John Hawle the younger, esquire, of Dertemouth..."* was granted letters of protection *"...staying in the King's service in the company of the King's esquire Richard Clideroe, the King's admiral of the fleet from the mouth of the Thames to the west, on the safe keeping of the sea."* [102]

Richard Clitheroe was a self-made man from the eponymous Lancashire town, who had prospered as a London merchant and whose talent for military logistics had made him a trusted servant of Richard II. He had displayed some opposition to Richard's overthrow and was consequently put on trial by Henry IV in 1400. There he defended himself so well as to gain Henry's unreserved favour and was soon appointed to various important and lucrative official positions. Being a respected merchant and administrator, and having also had some experience at sea, he was by 1406 perhaps the perfect candidate for election by the merchants as one of the admirals in the scheme for sub-contracting the defence of the seas which was put before the Long Parliament.* This arrangement, as we have seen, proved to be unsustainable and, although his initial appointment was to have run until Michaelmas in 1407, he in fact resigned it shortly before the end of the parliamentary session in December 1406. Hawley's appointment as his lieutenant therefore turned out to be of little or no practical significance.

With the notable exception of his brief incarceration in the Tower in 1406-7, the elder Hawley had managed to exploit his position as an indispensable paranaval commander, and skilfully to employ delaying tactics when claims were made against him in connection with his privateering activities. This had extended even to his dealings with the king and, when the father and son were together running the family business in the early 1400s, it is clear that they were still behaving in this way. Nor is there any indication of a change in attitude in the younger John after his father's death, but the extent to which the Crown was inclined to pursue enforcement of its commissions ordering restitution to the victims of privateering excesses varied considerably according to the political and diplomatic situation. In the early fifteenth century that situation became much more complicated and the relationship between the younger Hawley and the monarchs which he alternately served and annoyed was to see more extreme fluctuations than had even that of his father during most of his long career.

On November 20th 1407, as the elder John Hawley was about to proceed quietly into the last year of his life, Louis, duke of Orléans, the ally-turned-enemy of Henry IV, was mounting his horse in a Paris street when he was attacked by men acting under the orders of John, duke of Burgundy, who cut off both of his arms and killed

---

* *Nicholas Blackburn, Clitheroe's counterpart as admiral for the north under the scheme, was a prominent merchant in York.*

him. This bloody episode in the mortal feud between the houses of Orléans and Burgundy did not spark an immediate civil war in France but the tensions which it generated were such that it was only a matter of time before hostilities would break out. Events in France and the complex and rapidly changing diplomacy which they engendered, were to be the main focus of the foreign policy of the sick and distracted Henry IV for the rest of his reign and, thereafter, of his vigorous son, Henry V.

In 1410, Hawley, who never took on the extensive local role which his father had, either as mayor or burgess, was nonetheless elected, with the Gascon-born but long-time Dartmouth resident privateer, Edmund Arnold, to serve as MP for the borough. In November of that year, he was commissioned, with the mayor, to arrest no fewer than twenty-five men and bring them before the king in Chancery. The names of those to be arrested appear nowhere in the local records and one is described as being of Plymouth, and it is likely that the commission was in connection with privateering, although this was not specified. Hawley was presumably here being commissioned as an esquire who had appropriate, local connections, rather than as the incumbent of any particular office because such arrests would be of no relevance to his roles as escheator and feodary. What is clear is that, being an MP, and being entrusted with such duties on behalf of the Crown, he must have been of good standing at the time and was not himself subject to a similar commission for his arrest. This was to change just five months later.

Hawley's ships had, for some time, been acting in concert with those of two comparative newcomers to Dartmouth as a privateering base. John Prendergast, who is described as 'chivaler', and William Long of Rye, had recently been operating out of the port and, in March 1411, a commission for their arrest, along with that of Hawley, was issued at Westminster, because they were alleged to have committed:

"...divers depredations, spoliations and robberies and other damages and grievances... at sea on divers merchants, masters and mariners of ships of the parts of Flanders and other foreign parts...contrary to the treaties between the King and those of Flanders and other foreign parts and divers letters patent of safe conduct..."[103]

The reason for this sudden, apparent reversal in Hawley's official esteem was that, in the early months of 1411, one of the primary objectives of Henry's Council was to shore up the truces relating to Gascony and Flanders, whose support was deemed to be increasingly necessary in view of the events in France. The actions of the admiralty courts were being accelerated and intensified for urgent, diplomatic reasons which, as so often, overrode other, more parochial considerations. Similar diplomatic influences were to be seen at work again early in the following year. Jean, duke of Brittany had in 1411 entered into a ten-year truce with England, with specific provision for reparations in cases of piracy and, in February 1412, the sergeant at arms was instructed to seize a Breton ship, the *Seint Julien*, and her cargo, which had been captured by Hawley's men "...contrary to the form of the treaty between the King and his son, the duke of Brittany..."[104]

Henry V had a clear understanding of the priorities of naval warfare.

Illustration from Cassell's History
of England 1902

Not all disputes of this kind concerned enemies or former enemies. In 1412, Hawley was involved in a squabble with the owners and masters of a balinger, the *George of Paignton* which, as its name suggests, was based just ten miles up the coast from Dartmouth. The accounts of events given by the balinger's owners and her master, Thomas Rake, differ in detail from the version offered on behalf of Hawley, but the story was broadly as follows: Ships belonging to Thomas Carew and John Hawley had taken a Breton crayer off the coast of Brittany – with which dukedom a truce was then in force – on the grounds that she was freighted with wine and other merchandise which was alleged to be the property of French merchants and was therefore a legitimate prize. The argument on this occasion, however, was not concerned with the question as to whom the ship and cargo originally belonged, but rather with what happened to it subsequently. The captors put a prize crew of six aboard the crayer to bring her to Dartmouth but the Bretons overpowered them and killed four of them. The *George* then re-captured the vessel, taking her, with one of the surviving Englishmen*, to 'Torbay Jetty' in Paignton. Then, according to the claimants, John Hawley sent two of his balingers with a hundred men, *"armed and arrayed for war"*, who terrorised the crew of the *George* and took the crayer back to Dartmouth. Although this little local difficulty had been the subject of a claim made at Chancery, it was resolved locally soon after, when a four-man tribunal, with two members representing each side, agreed to split the prize between them.[105]

Hawley himself was sometimes asked to adjudicate on behalf of the Crown on similar matters around this time. Just three weeks after the death of Henry IV, on April 14th 1413, we see the Council ordering him and Thomas Carew to investigate what part of the cargoes recently captured in Breton vessels was the property of Breton merchants, to whom it should be restored, and what belonged to the *"King's enemies of France"* and could be retained as legitimate prizes of war.[106] They were also, in a second commission, asked to conduct similar examinations of other ships captured by men of Dartmouth and Fowey[107]. A third commission of the same date to Carew and the mayor is interesting and was, for Hawley, to prove troublesome. In this, Carew was instructed to appraise

---

* *What happened to the other survivor is not recorded.*

all tuns and pipes of wine from a Spanish balinger, the *Seint Croice*, which had been captured and were now in the hands of John Hawley[108]. The exclusion of Hawley from the third commission shows at least some superficial appreciation of the concept of conflict of interest but places what might be regarded as an unreasonable reliance on the integrity and impartiality of two individuals who were probably Hawley's friends or at least had personal reasons to maintain good relations with him.

In the *Seint Croice* incident, Hawley claimed to be operating under letters of marque granted in reprisal for piracies committed by men of Santander against a ship belonging to Margery, widow of John Russell of Coventry. This gave authority to seize any ship or merchandise of any merchant of Santander until Margery's claim was satisfied. The claim against Hawley, who had seized the ship when bad weather forced her into Dartmouth, hinged on the claimant's assertion that she was not of Santander. Hawley agreed to make full restitution in the following year, diplomatic considerations in relation to the truce with Spain having apparently pre-empted the continuing debate about the ship's port of origin.

A commission for Hawley's arrest was issued in August 1413 to Thomas Carew, the mayor and John Tiptot, a lieutenant of the admiral of England[109]. They were ordered to bring Hawley before the king in Chancery 'without delay'. It seems most likely that this was a final warning to settle the outstanding claim in relation to the *Seint Croice*, but it may have been for some other reason. Whether Hawley, who was again representing Dartmouth in parliament and, together with John Corp, had not long previously returned from Westminster, was obliged to make the journey again is not clear. It seems more likely that he simply agreed some kind of out-of-court settlement of whatever matter was involved.

In 1414, Hawley and Edmund Arnold travelled to Leicester to represent Dartmouth at the parliament which sat there in May and, apparently back in official favour, he was appointed escheator and feodary for Devon and Cornwall for life on November 27[th110]. He was clearly back on the right side of the law and the king's favour in 1415 when he was commissioned to investigate the whereabouts of ships stolen from Thomas Carew[111] and, more significantly, was granted royal letters of protection against any suits or commissions that might arise while he was absent as a member of the king's retinue during his first expedition to Normandy[112]. Henry's army sailed from Southampton in August 1415 and took Harfleur after a prolonged and costly siege. Although Harfleur was to be again contested, unsuccessfully, by the French, with a squadron of galleys and Genoese crossbowmen the following year, Henry had by then won his decisive victory at Agincourt. Hawley's role in this campaign is likely to have been in connection with Henry's troublesome maritime logistics[*] and it is unlikely that he was present at Agincourt. He nonetheless returned to Dartmouth on a triumphant note and managed to keep out of trouble for the next two years.

Once the French siege of Harfleur had been lifted and the galley fleets routed, Henry was ready to mount a full-scale invasion of Normandy and, in this connection,

---

[*] *Most of his soldiers were embarked on Dutch ships, for lack of English vessels.*

he summoned Hawley into his presence at Southampton in 1417. For some reason, Hawley failed to appear, affronting a king who was less inclined to being indulgent of his mariner subjects than his father had been, and he found his estates briefly forfeit in 1418. Henry did not, however, harbour the grudge for long and it was a rehabilitated Hawley who, in the summer of 1419, patrolled the Channel under the command of Sir Hugh Courtenay, heir to the earldom of Devon. This was a cruise quite unlike that undertaken by the elder Hawley and Thomas Norton in 1403, and there was no plunder to be had. Henry V had an understanding of what was required in naval strategy that his predecessors had completely lacked. Instead of allowing his subcontractor navy to patrol the sea as they pleased and to finance themselves by seizing ships and cargoes where they saw fit, he ensured that they were given specific instructions to conform to their part in a coherent overall strategy. So it was with Courtenay's force in 1419; they were instructed to cruise between Dieppe and Cherbourg and to blockade the Seine. This was a new and much more disciplined form of paranaval warfare.

It was to be in the following year, however, that the son of the old paranaval admiral was to reach the pinnacle of his own official maritime career. A revived alliance between France and Castile in June 1419, under which Castile undertook to provide forty ships and four thousand men, had given rise to a renewed naval challenge to England and it was in response to this threat that Hawley was recalled to serve under Courtenay, now earl of Devon, in 1420. What had become of the Hawley family's privateering flotilla in the twelve years since the death of the elder John is unknown, but it was *la Marie*, a ship owned by another Dartmouth man, Gervase Jakeman, and skippered by John Holman, that Hawley was, in February 1420, commissioned to man, provision and prepare for sea[113]. He sailed at the end of April, with a personal force of fifty men-at-arms and one hundred archers, as part of a larger force of five ships and ten balingers, embarking a military force totalling some five hundred men-at-arms and a thousand archers. He was one of the four commanders of this force, the others being Courtenay, William, Lord Botreaux and Hawley's old friend, fellow royal commissioner and 'chivaler', Thomas Carew. They were to patrol the Channel until the end of October but, in the event, they and the rest of Henry's now-powerful naval force were to have little to do. The threat posed by the Franco-Castilian alliance was suddenly removed by a reversal of the foreign policy of Castile, which resulted from a messy *coup d'état* there in July of that year.

Henry V had exercised tighter control of privateering and piracy than had any English monarch during the Hundred Years War but, on his premature death in 1422, this grip was relaxed. There is little evidence in the official record, however, of any sudden upsurge in privateering based in Dartmouth in the 1420s and the name of Hawley was to disappear from the proceedings of the admiralty courts for the first time in nearly fifty years. On his return from sea in the winter of 1420, Hawley started to spend more time in Cornwall and he served as a Justice of the Peace there for nine years from 1422. He was now able to enjoy the status of landed gentleman that his father had worked so hard to acquire and, although it is said that he continued to oversee privateering activities from Dartmouth, there is little direct evidence of this through the middle part of the decade. It may be that the repeated brushes with authority and the risk to his capital assets on the one side and the allure of genteel country life on the other had diminished his appetite for his old trade or that, for some reason – increased competition perhaps – it had become intrinsically less attractive. There was to be a marked increase in recorded privateering actions in Dartmouth in the early 1430s, but by then the third John Hawley seems to have settled down in the role of country squire and his involvement was limited to investigating transgressions in one or other official capacity.

There was, however, one incident before this which put him back into contention with the authorities for the last time and it was his old friend, Thomas Carew, who in November 1428 once more found himself among a group commissioned to arrest him. This probably related to the capture by Hawley's men of a Scottish ship which had been overtaken and plundered to the tune of two hundred and twenty pounds by a substantial English privateer force in 1427. Hawley had continued in the family tradition by failing to make prompt restitution and was called to account when he failed even to make good on the commitments that he had eventually been obliged to make. This was, however, no more than the kind of routine arrest warrant to which he had by now become accustomed and there is no evidence that he allowed it to disrupt his newly tranquil, respectable existence. Less than two years later we see his name again alongside that of Thomas Carew on the other side of a similar affair as, in April 1430, the two were commissioned to arrest and bring before the Council eighteen individuals in respect of unspecified charges.

The incident in 1427 marks the last known capture by a privateer of the house of Hawley and, although there probably were others later, they did not warrant official attention or record. The gentleman Hawley retained his links with Dartmouth in his last years but he had also become a familiar figure in Cornwall and at Westminster, where he represented Dartmouth for the last of the twelve occasions on which he was returned as MP for the borough in 1432. He continued to act as escheator and feodary and his expertise in maritime affairs was, from time to time, called upon until the last months of his life. In 1431 he was commissioned to seek out and restore to their owners three Breton vessels and their cargos which had been illegally seized by privateers operating out of Plymouth.

The changing political scene in France was once more causing acute concern and the balance of naval power in the Channel had turned strongly against England. Commissions of array in 1433 and 1436 called upon a number of men with familiar surnames to muster and organise the local defending forces against the threatened invasion. Among those answering the commission that: *"The men at arms, armed men and archers are to be arrayed by thousands, hundreds, twenties or otherwise and are to be mustered and inspected from time to time..."*[114] were Philip Courtenay, Nicholas Carew and John Hawley.

This more serene John Hawley evidently made more time in his twilight years to attend to his spiritual affairs than his father had and it is thought that his last sea voyage took him on a pilgrimage to the shrine of St James at Compostella. He died, probably in Cornwall, on May 8th 1436, just about one hundred years after his grandfather had made the journey into Dartmouth and laid the foundations of the Hawley enterprise in the mud by the fosse. The third John Hawley had two children by Margaret. Their son, Nicholas, died a young man in 1443 and the valuable estates passed to their daughter, Elizabeth, who had married John Copplestone, a lawyer, landowner and Devon MP. With this, the name of Dartmouth's most famous maritime family died out.

What manner of man?

The Hawleys were in no sense a dynasty. Dynasties are established by great leaders and the first John Hawley was unexceptional among his peers and is almost invisible to historians. The third of that name was resourceful, energetic, successful and sometimes controversial but, were it not for his famous father, would have been of little more than passing interest. As a family of Dartmouth merchant privateers, the three generations of Hawleys had a direct and contemporary parallel in the Asshendens. Thomas Asshenden accompanied Hawley on some of his more interesting exploits and, like Hawley, was returned as an MP for Dartmouth and combined privateering with a career in public service. His father, William, had served as mayor and his son, the second Thomas, like the younger Hawley, enjoyed the status of gentleman as a result of the efforts of his father and grandfather. And yet the name of Asshenden would be unknown to anyone but a specialist student of Dartmouth during this period.

The Hawley legend is the product of one man who, whilst manifestly exceptionally able and energetic, might seem to have differed little in most respects from contemporaries such as Asshenden, Benedict de Bottesana and John Corp. The association of the name of Hawley with Chaucer's shipman was first made in modern times and would not have been drawn were it not for the fact that, for some reason, the Hawley legend had passed down through the intervening five centuries. The suggested association derived from the legend and not the other way around.

Nor can the life of this particular Dartmouth privateer and local burgess have become the stuff of legend while his contemporaries vanished just because he has been the subject of research by a small band of historians. Here again, their researches followed the legend and, in some cases, their interest was aroused by the latterly suggested Chaucer connection. The narrative offered above summarises and, in some places, cautiously extrapolates from most of the reputable research which has been done on John Hawley and yet he remains a rather two-dimensional figure. The often dry material which has been assiduously deciphered, translated, transcribed and interpreted by scholars over the years tells of interesting exploits and hints at derring-do and at association with colourful personalities but it tells us almost nothing about the man himself. It is easy to see why this is so. Men of Hawley's time seldom wrote letters unless they had to and only the single letter from

Hawley to Henry IV survives. The biographers of most famous men of later times have access to sheaves of letters and other papers from which the personality of the subject pours forth. The would-be biographer of John Hawley has the one precious letter and must otherwise depend on the official accounts and orders penned by bored, overworked clerks who had neither time nor reason to elaborate on their terse communications.

The Calendar of the Patent Rolls and other such material provide us with a peephole through which we can view some aspects of Hawley's life, but it inevitably causes us to exaggerate the importance of that small part which we can see. We are therefore inclined to distort the picture and it is necessary for us to apply some kind of corrective lens to the story which results if we are to make a more balanced assessment of him. The lack of positive evidence necessitates a process of forensic inference which must often focus not on what information is available but on what is missing. What, then, is missing? What manner of man was the second John Hawley and why did he become a legendary figure?

The story of Hawley the privateer is illustrated – and probably particularly distorted – by the nature of the record. We see many detailed reports of seizures of neutral vessels and their cargoes but the various Castilian, Piedmontese, Flemish and Dutch merchants making claims for restitution are, in all likelihood, just a minority of those who fell foul of Hawley's men, and sit disconsolately on the tip of a much larger iceberg. Notable by their near absence are records of legitimate captures and prizes of war; French and Breton names appear only during intervals of truce and seldom even then. We cannot easily estimate what portion of captures by the Dartmouth privateers the claims of neutrals represent but this question is important if we are to draw conclusions as to whether Hawley really was the privateer that he purported to be or was merely a pirate who preyed upon the easiest and most lucrative targets that presented themselves.

We may incline to the judgement that he was a privateer because official records in this period usually report the unusual or irregular and there was always much more going on which was left unrecorded. It is also evident that the claimants were able to press their cases and often won. When they did, Hawley was forced to waste significant amounts of time and, presumably, money in retrieving and delivering the captured goods or otherwise making amends. As long as there was any semblance of a system of redress through the courts – which usually there was – raiding neutral shipping was simply too troublesome a business for it to be a worthwhile mainstay of a commercial venture. By contrast, a successful raid on a significant enemy asset could be fabulously profitable and, in a time of war, legitimate privateering must have been a much more attractive and profitable business than piracy.

Neutral ships did often carry enemy cargos, however, and the capture of enemy goods from neutral ships was more than just a potentially lucrative sideline, so the courts which adjudicated on cases relating to seizures by privateers necessarily understood that the rules were such that a certain amount of collateral damage was inevitable. Provided, however, that restitution was made where appropriate, there should have been no lasting stain on the character of the privateers who were called to account. John Hawley's reputation survived many such cases intact, although he was always litigious and often slow to make recompense when the judgement went against him, and it seems unlikely that it would have remained untarnished if he had not abided by the rules most of the time. There must have been many who had ample reason to fear and loathe Hawley and they doubtless would be inclined to regard him as a common pirate. The balance of the evidence, however, suggests that he was not a pirate or, at least, that it was not his general intention to be one.

Also missing from the official record, except in a very few and exceptional cases, are the 'men of John Hawley', the 'divers lieges' and 'evildoers' and other such, who were so often mentioned generically in the records but seldom individually, presumably because the circumstances had made it impossible to identify them. It was, however, relatively easy to recognise ships and in most cases it was the ships' owners, not the crews, or even the masters, who were called to account. The reason why this should be so is obvious enough. The plaintiffs in these cases were invariably seeking recompense, not retribution, and it was to the ships' owners that they naturally turned. The owners were easily identifiable, could generally be held responsible at law for the deeds of their employees and, most crucially, were wealthy enough to make compensation. The pragmatic recognition that the existence of a state of war might potentially provide justification for actions which might, in other circumstances, be regarded as criminal meant that these cases were, in essence, claims for civil damages, even where criminality was implied. This meant that John Hawley would find himself implicitly and almost routinely accused of piracy in relation to deeds over which he had no direct control and which were usually committed in his absence.

This raises the question of how and to what degree privateer bosses such as Hawley, and William Smale before him, should be held responsible for the actions of their skippers and crews. There is some evidence to suggest either that Hawley was careful to agree rules of conduct with the masters of his ships, or that he did not appoint anyone to such a post unless he already had experience sufficient to make such judgements wisely. In the well-documented case of the crayers which escaped at Audierne, we see Perkyn Dobyn, skipper of the *Trinity*, behaving in a professional and circumspect manner and it is apparent from his actions that he was making important legal, as well as nautical and tactical, judgements as part of his job. The relationship between Hawley and Dobyn must have required a high degree of mutual trust. Hawley was not only entrusting Dobyn with the care of a substantial capital asset but also with his reputation. Dobyn, in turn, would have to hope that Hawley would support him if he were to find himself in trouble as a result of his actions. In this light, we can see that Hawley's real responsibility at law derived from his responsibility to ensure that his ships' masters were professionally competent and that that competence extended to an ability to justify their independent actions, at law, should the need arise.

It might seem from the record that, in his privateering, Hawley was always the victor and never the victim, but this is probably misleading. The nature of the accessible records is such that there would seldom be reason for his losses to be recorded but it is inconceivable that he had none and it is likely that he had his fair share. Our knowledge of his ships is fragmentary. We know the names and general nature of some of them and it is clear that he must have owned several, but we do not know how many at any time. We know nothing of losses and additions to his fleet and so the score sheet for his high-stakes and risky trade is not accessible. In this connection, the example of the fight at Audierne is interesting. If we accept Richard Scoce's testimony that there was a fight and that it was as he described it, we see what a scrappy and dangerous business this kind of action was. Although, in this instance, it seems that the privateer force was ultimately overwhelming, the Bretons nonetheless put up stiff resistance and John Cornyssh died as a result. Hawley's men must on occasion have been involved in other, less unequal actions in which crewmen and ships were lost.

These, though, were dangers where were faced by his crews and not, for the most part, by Hawley himself. We have no evidence of Hawley ever having gone to sea as master of a vessel and it is quite likely that he never did. He may have ventured out in that capacity as a young man in order that he could learn his trade but it is much more likely that he would have put in his sea time under the supervision of an experienced skipper and, by the time we see him scouring the seas with Thomas Norton, it is as a quasi-admiral, not a ship's master. So, however alluring the notion of Hawley as the swashbuckling master mariner may be, it is not an image of him which is consistent with the available evidence. For most of his privateering career he played the role of shore-based privateer admiral, organising the affairs of his small fleet with consummate skill, whilst simultaneously running the town, negotiating with the authorities and defending the actions of his men in court. He was far more valuable in this capacity than ever he would have been as master of a single ship or even as the seagoing commander of a small squadron. He employed the likes of Perkyn Dobyn to do that.

Hawley's genius as a privateer lay in his understanding of how paranaval admirals such as he could profitably exploit the failure of successive kings to come to grips with the problem of protecting the seas. It was always, however, a hazardous and contentious business and the tenacity and obstinacy that he displayed in his dealings with the world in general and the Crown in particular were the product not only of an irrepressible personality but of an appreciation of how much he always had to lose. He was running a dangerous enterprise in dangerous times and had become conditioned by experience never to concede a point or to give ground unless and until he was forced to. He was litigious because he had to be.

It is sometimes said of the merchant classes of the late Middle Ages that their intellectual horizons were limited by the constraints which the social class system placed upon them and that they were generally fortunate to be able to operate within a world which, by comparison with that which their social betters inhabited, was comfortable and predictable. If this was true of merchants in general, it was not true of shipowners, whose capital assets were nearly always at risk, and even less true of privateer merchants, who deliberately put large portions of their fortunes in harm's way on a routine basis. Hawley was a risk taker but he also had an understanding of the ways in which he could diversify his risk or tip the odds in his favour. Being mayor, MP and a landowner all made his position more secure and at the same time opened up new opportunities. His acquisition of the Tresilian estates diversified his business risk and brought social recognition, while his services to the Crown earned him a coat of arms and some political influence where he most needed it. But late medieval English society, long accustomed to honouring land-based soldiery with knighthoods and more, had not come to terms with the idea of a sea-going equivalent. This, in turn, meant that the official dealings of even the most public-spirited and respectable of the privateer bosses were likely to be more litigious and fraught than were those of their knightly betters.

Hawley was not alone in combining important civic responsibilities with the role of privateer admiral – Thomas Norton of Bristol, with whom Hawley cruised in the autumn of 1403, was of a similar mould – but Hawley was perhaps the most complete example of the type. He was the dominant figure among a small group of shipowner burgesses which ran Dartmouth for almost half a century and he energetically promoted the interests of this group, and of the town, at a national level. The membership of the group changed over the years but Hawley was a constant and dominant presence.

There can be no doubt that Hawley was driven, and powerfully driven, by self interest. He became extremely wealthy and never missed an opportunity to increase his wealth and social standing, but he understood the value of collaboration and he seems to have run both his business and the town in a spirit of charismatic mutualism. Such was his natural authority that it is easy to imagine Dartmouth in years around the turn of the fifteenth century as a kind of 'company town', with Hawley as mayor and *de facto* chief executive of 'Hawley & Co.' In a small town whose principal business was risky, volatile and not susceptible to precise accounting and record-keeping, and where the tax regime was less than rigorous, the benefits of 'trickle-down' economics did not need to trickle very far in order to engender a widespread feeling of prosperity. As Hawley prospered, so did everyone else. By the end of the fourteenth century he had achieved every economic, political and social distinction that was available to him within the constraints of the medieval class system, and it might reasonably have been expected that he would retire to enjoy the fruits of his labours. This might have been so for another man at another time, but Hawley did the opposite. He went to sea to fight.

In the first years of the fifteenth century, as the undeclared war at sea intensified, Dartmouth was again of acute strategic importance and the name of the town was by now synonymous with Hawley. This tightly-knit community now came under a direct and substantial threat and it was perhaps inevitable that, having achieved all his other material and social ambitions, and in search, perhaps, of some kind of transcendent glory, he would don his armour and ride, or more likely sail, to its defence. The king and the people of Dartmouth, in turn, naturally turned to him for leadership. He was surrounded by very competent men, such as John Corp, but none had his breadth of experience or natural authority and he was the obvious local leader in this time of crisis. We do not know where he was or what he was doing while the local militia was slaughtering the Breton soldiery at Blackpool but it is easy to imagine how, in their triumph, the defenders might enthusiastically have hailed the chief when the danger passed. It is at such times that legends are born.

Hawley, inevitably, was not a hero to everyone and his imprisonment in the Tower in 1406-7, in which his local celebrity perhaps worked to his disadvantage by highlighting his value as an economic hostage, suggests that the ruling classes of his time were reluctant to acclaim men of his social class and of his controversial profession.

Hawley's memorial brass in St. Saviour's church perhaps depicts the kind of man he would have liked to have been. Brass memorials of this kind in the early fifteenth century were all made to order by workshops in London by men who had probably never seen the people whose effigies they were engraving. The inscription, at least, is most likely posthumous and, although the elder John may well have commissioned and approved the memorial to himself and his wives, it is also possible that his son ordered it and specified the general nature of the image to be executed. The elder John would certainly have worn armour from time to time but it is highly unlikely that he would ever have appeared as depicted. The only land battle in which he may have been involved was at Blackpool and, although it is just possible that the old man might have turned up for this in full mail and plate armour and riding a heavy horse, this seems very unlikely. The fact that the memorial shows him holding Joan by the hand, while Alice stands alone in a pious pose, may be significant. The first churchwarden's accounts for St. Saviours in 1430 show:

"For the expenses of keeping the obit of John Hawley, and Johanna his wife and of Margaret Hawley in bread, wine and beer, with priests and bell ringers…..3s. 4d."[115]

Poor Alice, of whom we know nothing but the date of her death, seems to have been ignored by her family after her passing. Perhaps the elder John never got on with his second wife, or maybe her stepson resented her. As with so much of the human side of the Hawley men, we will never know.

The younger John's inscription on his father's memorial, however, likely reflects the judgement of the people of Dartmouth. He is described there as *"venerabilis vir"*, a more respectful rendering, perhaps, of what Chaucer said, ironically, of his Shipman and of what Hawley's contemporaries may have said, more informally and sincerely, of him…

"And certainly he was a good felawe."

Chapter Seven:

John Hawley and Chaucer's Shipman

Chaucer's *Canterbury Tales* is one of the most completely, minutely and frequently analysed literary works of all time. Chaucer scholars, medievalists and medievalist/Chaucer scholars have engaged in lively debates which have ranged worldwide and spanned many generations, on every aspect of its provenance and meaning. The literature *about* Chaucer is vast and its volume completely dwarfs that of the literature *of* Chaucer. Within this substantial body of scholarship there developed, in the early part of the twentieth century, a significant field of study whose practitioners have tried to ascribe specific identities to the more prominent pilgrims described by Chaucer in the general prologue. The *Canterbury Tales* is a multi-layered and deeply satirical work in which Chaucer identifies some real London people. In the prologue to the Cook's Tale, he names the host of the Tabard, the inn in Southwark from which the pilgrims depart on their journey to Canterbury, as Harry Bailly and the cook as Roger Hodge of Ware. In the general prologue, he draws character sketches of the other pilgrims, implicitly inviting his contemporary audience to speculate as to the veiled identities of some of them. Whether or not contemporary readers commonly took up the invitation, modern scholars have done so with gusto, with some wonderfully erudite and entertaining results.

This is a field into which those whose interest is purely historical wander at their peril but the name of John Hawley has been so often and so carelessly associated with the Shipman pilgrim that this essay on Hawley would justifiably be found wanting if it did not include some attempt to examine whether or not this association might be plausible. Entire monographs have been dedicated to the analysis of individual pilgrims, perhaps the best-known recent example of this genre being Terry Jones' *Chaucer's Knight*. The Shipman has nowhere been subjected to such detailed scrutiny, but Margaret Galway's 1939 contribution to *The Modern Language Review: "Chaucer's Shipman in Real Life"* offers a particular historical interpretation.

Any attempt to identify the individuals to which Chaucer may have been alluding must consider, in addition to the poet's likely artistic and satirical intentions, the audience for which he was writing and the subjects of which both he and his audience would or could have had knowledge. Also, given that any personalised satire tends to be very specific to a time and place, that is to say, the time and place of the writer and the intended audience, it is important to know when the portrait in question was written. Satire, arguably, is a dish best served hot.

Unfortunately, although great efforts have been made to resolve these questions, none can be answered with any high degree of certainty. The author lays no claim whatever to specialist knowledge of Chaucer and his writings and can contribute little to the literary debate but the reader should be made aware of the assumptions on which the historical interpretation offered here is based. The current received wisdom as to the chronology of Chaucer's work on the *Canterbury Tales* is that he started it around 1387 and there can be no doubt that it constituted the greater part of his writing thereafter, until his death in 1400. The work was unfinished when he died and was assembled from many fragments for publication posthumously. As regards the intended audience, the template used here is that offered by Derek Pearsall in his *Life of Geoffrey Chaucer*, viz.: *"...a miscellaneous company of lettered London men, to be appropriately scandalized..."*[116]

The approach taken to analysis of the pilgrims in the works of Terry Jones and Margaret Galway cited above is similar in some ways but different in one crucial respect. Both examine the descriptions of their subjects in the general prologue line by line and draw inferences as to their identities from the detail but, whereas Galway makes a direct leap from the detailed description to a specific individual, Jones identifies the subject as a very particular type and leaves open the possibility that the audience was being invited to extrapolate, by association, from this allusion to a fairly specific type of man, to a very specific individual who might have warranted a somewhat different personal description.

In Jones' very persuasive analysis of the Knight, the satirical reference may thus be seen as having been intended to be doubly oblique. In the first place, he argues that what appears, from a superficial reading of the text, to be a straightforward description of a gallant model of chivalric virtue is in fact a complex satire on the anonymous English mercenaries who fought exclusively for foreign kings and princes. The best-known contemporary mercenary, and a man whose name would have been known to anyone in Chaucer's immediate audience, was Sir John Hawkwood, who, with his huge mercenary army, the White Company, plagued the various states of Italy, back and forth, for a generation. The man described with such complex irony

The Cook – Roger of Ware was not a fictional character.

Illustration from an edition of 'The Canterbury Tales' Ellesmere manuscript c 1410

is an ordinary, anonymous and thereby doubly sinister mercenary soldier, identifiable not least by his *'bismotered'* [soiled] jupon, devoid of any livery; but the image was more likely intended to be interpreted by his audience as a satire on Hawkwood, whose battledress would no doubt have been pristine and who would be operating at a more elevated and politically interesting level. Hawkwood had risen through the ranks as an archer and man-at-arms and so, while the description would not have fitted him at the time of writing, it would have done in the past. It should also be noted that Chaucer had personal knowledge of Hawkwood; he met and attended negotiations with him in Milan in 1378, as esquire to an envoy of Richard II.*

The irony in the description of the Shipman is barely concealed. The *"good felawe"* is clearly a rogue, albeit possibly an affable one, and his lack of scruple in his business and ruthlessness in combat are also laid out clearly enough. The exact nature of his trade is less clear. He is described as being involved in the Bordeaux wine trade, which is consistent with his being based in Dartmouth, but this would have applied to so many seamen that this adds little or nothing by which we might identify what manner of man the sketch is intended to represent. He could be a simple merchant mariner who is sometimes called upon to fight or a merchant mariner-cum-privateer, for whom fighting would have been a stock in trade. Some scholars have lit upon the name of his ship, the *Maudelayne* as providing the vital clue to his identity, as does Margaret Galway, whose analysis warrants some examination here.

Galway takes a literal, line-by-line approach to analysing the description of the Shipman in the general prologue and concludes that it makes a quite direct allusion to one John Piers, a Basque seaman who settled in England and lived for a time in Teignmouth. She draws an elaborate and scholarly argument in favour of Piers as the Shipman, a principal plank of which is his capture, in September 1383, of a vessel called the *Magdaleyn*, whose crew were all killed. This, she says, was a subject of London gossip in 1384, in plenty of time for Chaucer to be alluding to it in the

---

* *Jones' view of the Knight as a possible satire of Hawkwood is at least tacitly supported by his modern biographer, Frances Stonor Saunders, in* Hawkwood – Diabolical Englishman.

Canterbury Tales. The argument that the Shipman was a Basque, and thereby the only foreigner among the pilgrims assembled at the Tabard, is based on two strands of evidence from the text. Firstly, she argues that Spanish seamen were notorious for throwing the crews of captured ships overboard, while the English were not. She then suggests that the fact that the Shipman's detailed knowledge extends explicitly to "Spayne" and, in particular, to the Mediterranean coast of Spain, to which English seamen seldom, if ever, ventured, strongly suggests that he was a Spaniard. The latter point is an interesting one but, whilst we might imagine that Chaucer might not have been above exploiting anti-Spanish sentiments in his audience and may have made such an allusion for that effect, the notion that English seamen were so little inclined to dispose of their captives in the way described as to contrast sharply with the alleged Spanish practice hardly stands up to scrutiny. William Smale's men displayed no more scruple when throwing defeated seamen over the side in 1346 or 1360 than had Edward III's troops in 1340 in the heat of the Battle of Sluys.

John Piers is a name which appears quite frequently among seamen of this period. There was a John Piers living in Hardness in the 1350s and one such – probably the same man – was listed, with his wife Juliana, in the Dartmouth poll tax returns of 1377. This is probably the man to whom Galway herself makes reference as one of that name who was "appointed chief ship searcher" in Dartmouth in 1386 and was likely the skipper of Hawley's *'barge of Mortrigo'* which was involved in the events of that year which led to the Roches vs. Hawley trial. Yet another John Piers, who might conceivably be the one to which Galway refers, lodged a claim against Hawley and Norton in respect of seizure of his Castilian vessel, the *'Seynte Piere'* during the cruise of 1403. It is easy to see, at a time when people were often referred to by their Christian names and places of residence, that variations on 'Jean-Pierre' would have been common enough, but Galway has no doubts about the identity of her man and tenaciously works through every line of the general prologue description, indicating how he fills the bill in every respect.

While she makes much of his Spanishness and is at pains to explain why this would fit into Chaucer's satirical scheme, she is generally dismissive of the mention of Dartmouth as the sailor's home and, perhaps rather implausibly, turns her own argument on its head thus:

> *"This passing mention of Dartmouth, and the existence there in the poet's time of a vessel called the Magdaleyne, probably owned by the great John Hawley, have given rise to the well-known theory that the Shipman was one of the masters of the Dartmouth Magdaleyne, an obscure sailor named Peter Risshenden. But the second line is not really a satisfactory foundation for that theory. Admittedly it suggests that the Shipman might have been of*

Sir John Hawkwood – English mercenary general and likely object of Chaucer's satirical treatment of the Knight.

Engraving based on an Italian fresco

Dartmouth, but it also deliberately refrains from saying that he was. In connection with this odd procedure we should remember a fact well known to Chaucer's contemporaries; namely, that Spanish sailors dreaded the mere name of John Hawley and had no worse enemies in England than his henchmen. And the description of the Shipman gives us reason to suspect that Spain was his native land. Possibly therefore the suggestion that perhaps he was of Dartmouth is a mild Chaucerian joke, an ironic relegation of him to the last English port he would have been likely to choose, or be allowed, to live in."[117]

The reverence in which Chaucer is held is such that every word of these character portraits is assumed to have some literal and precise significance and also to enclose some deeper allegorical meaning. This approach is often justified but can be dangerous. Galway, for example, perhaps works rather too hard to establish that the physical description of the Shipman has unmistakeable Basque characteristics:

"The Basques, the codex tells us, wore 'short mantles...cut at the knee'; their long outer cloaks were 'woollen' and 'black', and each landsman at least had a horn hung 'round his neck', as the Shipman had a dagger 'hangynge on a laas...aboute his nekke'. A writer of the sixteenth century recorded that the Basques invariably carried a small weapon."[118]

Here and elsewhere in her engaging essay, Galway's argument seems to become somewhat over-extended and is perhaps weighed down under the burden of her erudition. On this latter point, it can be stated with reasonable confidence that the garb and personal armament described would have been recognisable as those of a common English seaman of the time and the *"daggere hangynge on a laas"* might well have served both as a weapon and a day-to-day boat knife. One Devon historian, writing in 1880, offers a more straightforward perspective and, in his detailed description of the cloth, rather undermines the Basque clothing theory:

"Doubtless to go on a pilgrimage to Canterbury the schipman would don his best attire; but the "gown of faldyng to the knee" is simply graphic. Faldyng was a course frieze cloth of a very unfinished sort, and very likely, in this instance, to have been made in one of the many Devonshire looms. Large quantities of this cloth were made in England and exported to other countries. The long blue gown, to the knee, tightened at the waist, is no longer the costume of sailors generally, but it is still to be seen occasionally among the fishermen and others in the little seaside villages in Devon and Cornwall and perhaps elsewhere"[119]

In all, this seems to be a fairly straightforward portrait of a contemporary seaman from which Galway has tried to draw too many inferences. But, if her theory about John Piers is to be rejected, what is the Shipman, who might he be and why does Chaucer have him join the pilgrims?

Some Chaucer scholars have puzzled over the inclusion of the Shipman in the *Canterbury Tales*. The Shipman's story lacks a prologue or epilogue and generally looks as if it was added as an afterthought. Why Chaucer chose to cast a shipman as one of his pilgrims is not apparent from the narrative; *The Shipman's Tale* itself, a story of marital infidelity and ecclesiastical iniquity, hardly resonates with the character and likely experience of the man he describes. There is strong textual evidence, in fact, that it was originally written for the Wife of Bath or, at any rate, a female pilgrim and later allocated to the Shipman in a rather arbitrary fashion. The other pilgrims, for the most part, fit neatly into a pattern of generic satires of the three medieval social 'estates' – the clergy, the aristocracy and the peasantry, although, by Chaucer's time, this pattern had become sufficiently frayed that the third estate might more aptly be described as 'the rest'. The Merchant and the Wife of Bath fit less comfortably into the traditional pattern but arguably the most outstanding misfit is the Shipman. Merchants and the non-aristocratic well-to-do were easily enough understood when Chaucer was writing but the role of shipmen such as Hawley was ill-defined and controversial. Chaucer himself came from a merchant family but had slotted into court life easily enough and his dealings with sailors, from those ordinary mariners who had routinely transported him on his diplomatic voyages, to the burgesses of Dartmouth with whom he had more substantial dealings, in all likelihood left him regarding them as, at best, rough diamonds and, at worst, something much more sinister. This is exactly the image conveyed by the Shipman, whose inclusion perhaps reflects nothing more than the poet's reluctance to let good material go to waste. He had met these people; they were colourful, controversial and ideal objects of satire.

Margaret Galway makes much of the uncertainty implied by *"For aught I woot…"* as regards the Shipman's home port and draws her own conclusions about what this implies. This phrase should maybe give us some pause in identifying him as a Dartmothian but it would be perverse to think that the reference to the town has no significance. The Dartmouth men had a particular reputation

The Shipman – More Perkyn Dobyn than John Hawley.
Illustration from an edition of 'The Canterbury Tales' Ellesmere
manuscript c 1410

at the time and, having had personal dealings with them, Chaucer would naturally have mentioned the port as a way of introducing the generic type, with which his immediate audience would also have had some familiarity.

A literal reading of the text raises another question. If any significance is attributed to the word 'If' in the line *"If that he faught, and hadde the hyer honde"*, the man described is not an out-and-out privateer. Most of Hawley's men did fight on quite a regular basis; there was no 'if' about it. Even they, however, often turned to more peaceable activities in time of truce, while all merchant seamen at the time had to be prepared to fight should the need arise – which it often did. We should perhaps, therefore, not worry unduly about the 'If' and just accept the most obvious implication that this is a portrait of a Dartmouth merchant mariner-cum-privateer.

The portrayal of the Shipman cannot, however, be regarded as a realistic and literal description of John Hawley himself. If we examine the evidence in the Galway style of literal dissection, that idea can be quickly dispelled. Hawley was certainly of Dartmouth and was thereby *"wonynge fer by weste"* but he rode all over the country for years and must have been a competent horseman. He was very wealthy and would certainly not have ridden a 'rouncy' – a common hackney horse or nag. He may well have carried a dagger on a lanyard and worn an ordinary seaman's practical clothing when at sea and he lived a sufficiently outdoor lifestyle that we have no difficulty in imagining him with a tanned or weather-beaten complexion. Most of the time, however, he would have been attired as a wealthy merchant and eminent local burgess.

He may have had some basic understanding of tides, streams and *"lodemenage"*, and have spent enough time at sea to have known a few creeks and havens. He was familiar with the coast of Brittany in general and St Mathieu in particular, but his knowledge would not have extended much beyond that in any detail and he was probably a complete stranger to both Jutland and Cartagena. He was, in short, not the seasoned, professional ship's master described. If we looking for a known figure who would have fitted this description in almost every way, we could point with some confidence to William Smale, John Weston, Michael Kykard, Peter Risshenden, Perkyn Dobyn or, indeed, Dartmouth's John Piers.

As regards the *Maudelayne,* there were several ships of that name in Dartmouth over the years, one of which was skippered by Peter Risshenden and one of which may have been owned by Hawley, but the simple truth is that there were too many *Maudelaynes* for the reference to be of much use in identifying the master or owner described. If the name has a significance it is, for now, obscure. Most ships of the time bore the names of saints and *Maudelayne,* with all its various spellings, was a favourite, so a more irreverent reader of the text might suggest that the poet may simply have hit upon Maudelayne when casting around for a common ship's name which would rhyme with *"Spayne".*

Ray Freeman has suggested that Chaucer would have been aware of the reputation of William Smale and that, if the Shipman was modelled on any individual; he was a more likely candidate than Hawley.[120] This observation is persuasive insofar as Smale was a professional seaman and his name, at least, was associated with two documented instances, in 1346 and 1360, in which defeated mariners were thrown into the sea. He had by then become affluent and eminent as a merchant and mayor and would have projected a different image but the description would probably have fitted him near-perfectly at an earlier time. A younger Smale is certainly, in terms of the literal description of the Shipman by itself, a stronger candidate than Hawley. He was, however, not a close contemporary of Chaucer and had been dead for perhaps thirty years when the *Canterbury Tales* were being written, so his name and reputation would probably not have been familiar to the poet's intended audience.

The technique of literal, line-by-line dissection in search of the Shipman, does not, however, really produce convincing answers. As targets for satirical allusions likely to be of interest to a London-based, literate audience of esquires, administrators and the like, Smale, Weston, Kykard, Risshenden, Dobyn and even John Piers look like dead-ends. In specifically naming the real-life Harry Bailly and Roger of Ware, Chaucer was inviting his audience to think that at least some of the other character sketches referred to real people but, insofar as the deeper purpose of the characterisations was a biting social satire, it makes little sense to think that he would then go on to describe these individuals directly, in great detail and in all but name. To Chaucer's well-to-do and worldly-wise audience, the likes of the grubby, mercenary knight and the shifty seaman were but the instruments of the people who really interested them. If the character sketches were intended to be anything more than depictions of generic types, it was surely at the relevant, famous contemporaries that Chaucer's satirical darts were aimed.

By the time that Hawley was ensuring the survival of his legend at Blackpool in 1404, Chaucer had been dead for three and a half years but, even when the *Canterbury Tales* were being written, there was no other Dartmouth man who had anything like Hawley's celebrity or, more pertinently, notoriety. The *'Batel of Hawley's barge'* took place a year before Chaucer resigned from the Customs and settled down in Greenwich to begin writing his masterpiece and the resulting, sensational trial of *Roches vs. Hawley*, with its accusations of piracy and treason, was going on just six miles away in Westminster for most of the time he was writing it. The men of Chaucer's circle would have been aware of the trial and were, no doubt, enjoying it. To these people and at that time, the notion of a Dartmouth shipman, however humble the image portrayed, would have been synonymous with only one name. The description of the Shipman is of a professional mariner like John Piers or Perkyn Dobyn but the satirical allusion, so central to the social commentary of the *Canterbury Tales*, must surely have been to their famous boss – John Hawley.

The Shipman astride his "rouncy" – an unlikely mount for John Hawley.
Woodcut of the Shipman from Pynson's 1492 edition of Chaucer's 'Canterbury Tales'

Epilogue

Men of affairs who are fated to live in tempestuous times seldom die of old age with their life's work complete, their heirs competently carrying on their business and the causes which they have championed in the full flood of success. John Hawley was therefore unusually fortunate in that he lived for about sixty-eight years – a very respectable span for the times – and was succeeded by a notably competent son who carried on his work in a style of which he would have approved.

The Hawley family fortunes were unquestionably at their zenith when he died and Dartmouth was as prosperous and important a port as it was ever to be. The war with France had already lasted seventy-one years and, although it was to continue for another forty-five and end in defeat, the high point of English fortunes was yet to come.

After his victory at Agincourt, Henry V concentrated his military efforts in Normandy. In the summer of 1419, by which time his army had successfully laid siege to Caen, Falaise, Cherbourg and Rouen, he had taken it all. The focus of the war thus moved eastwards and, although the Dartmouth privateers had seldom operated to the east of the Cherbourg peninsula during the life of the elder Hawley, it was here that the younger John was patrolling with Sir Hugh Courtenay in 1419. For Dartmouth as a privateer stronghold this was to be the beginning of the end.

Emboldened by a series of victories and by divisions in the French camp, where the houses of Valois and Burgundy continued to feud, Henry pressed his claim to the throne of France, a crown which he came close to achieving when, together with the Burgundy faction, he forced the Treaty of Troyes on the deranged and ailing Charles VI in 1420. Whether this could ever have been the basis of a lasting peace in France is very doubtful but, when Henry became ill while besieging the fortified town of Meaux in August 1422 and died two weeks short of his thirty-fifth birthday, any prospect of an English king thus imposing his will died with him.

English military might still prevailed in France for another seven years and the war was to continue for three decades and more but, when Joan of Arc raised the siege of Orléans in May 1429, the tide finally turned. The coronation of Charles VII at Rheims in 1429 was an affront to English claims to the throne and, in December 1431, the ten year-old Henry VI was taken to Paris, there to be crowned king of France by an English bishop. Under the Treaty of Troyes, his claim to the succession might have been sustainable but, when Philip of Burgundy changed sides in 1435, any significant support for the treaty which may have remained in France was lost.

A series of English defeats followed. Dieppe and Harfleur were lost in 1435, to be followed by Paris in the following year. The English fought hard to hold the line but were finding it increasingly difficult to retain Normandy. A final diplomatic effort to halt the war resulted in the truce of Tours in 1344, as a part of which arrangement Henry VI was to marry Margaret of Anjou, a niece of Charles VII. This was, however, to prove but a temporary respite and, by the summer of 1450, the English had been driven out of Normandy, retaining only Calais.

The privateers of Dartmouth had their last hurrah in 1449 under the leadership of Robert Wenyngton, who followed in the Hawley tradition of combining privateering with municipal office, being elected the town's mayor in 1448 and 1456. Having been commissioned in April 1449 to serve the king at sea and clear it of pirates, he duly sailed with a small fleet which soon took two Breton vessels which were sailing out of Flanders. Then, exhibiting commendable seamanship but a lack of diplomatic foresight, he parlayed with and then captured a substantial fleet of ships from Lubeck, Prussia, Holland and Flanders – all neutrals – which he took the to the Isle of Wight, from where he sent a letter to the king's council, asking what he should do with them. Wenyngton was within his rights under the old rules, by which he could stop and search neutral vessels and fight them if they offered resistance, but the tide of diplomacy was by now flowing strongly against him and the end result was that the Crown later had to pay substantial compensation to the duke of Burgundy is respect of his actions.

In March 1452, in what must have been one of the last orders of its kind issued during the Hundred Years War, Henry VI called upon shipowners of Dartmouth and other ports to assemble at Sandwich in order to provide support in the defence of Calais against French attacks. Calais was saved but, with the French ascendancy established, it was only a matter of time before Aquitaine, which had not been the subject of serious dispute since 1413, would also come under attack. In 1451, the French overran most of the duchy and captured Bordeaux. The English and their supporters briefly regained control of the city in 1452 but, when the earl of Shrewsbury, leader of the defending forces at the battle of Castillon, fell to French cannon fire and his heavily outnumbered troops were routed on July 17th 1453, the war with France was finally lost.

The wine trade with England was too important to Bordeaux for it to cease altogether, even after the city was finally surrendered to the French in 1453. During the brief restoration of English rule in the autumn of 1452 full-scale exports of wine were resumed, with fully-laden ships taking advantage of the comparative safety of the sea routes at that time. One of the last ships to sail under this brief resumption of the traditional trade arrived in Hull in April 1453, laden with fully three hundred and fifty-four tuns of wine. It is touchingly evocative of what was to prove to be the end of an era that she was the *Trinity of Dartmouth*.

England was soon to descend into civil war and, under Edward IV, the cogs and their bowmen no longer reigned supreme, as specialist warships were commissioned whose sides were pierced for guns. Gascony was lost and foreign trade came increasingly under the control of the merchant companies of London. The days of the cogs and the merchant-privateers were over and Dartmouth was never to regain the prominence which it enjoyed under the Hawleys.

Timeline

1147:   Ships assemble at Dartmouth prior to the Second Crusade

1153:   Marriage of Henry II to Eleanor of Aquitaine

1166:   Townstal passes to the Fitz Stephan family

1224:   Henry III arrests Dartmouth ships for royal service

1250:   Clifton-Dartmouth-Hardness a *de facto* borough under Fitz Stephans

1253:   Henry III arrests Dartmouth ships for campaign in Gascony

1264:   Sea fight between men of Dartmouth and men of Lyme

1270:   Henry III grants freedoms to *"the burgesses and merchants of Dertemue"*

1286:   Dartmouth residents petition Edward I regarding building of church at Clifton

1326:   Isabella and Mortimer overthrow Edward II

1327:   Edward III crowned at age of fourteen

1327:   Nicholas of Tewkesbury gifts Dartmouth to Edward III

1328:   Death of Charles IV of France leaves uncertain succession

1337:   Philip VI declares Aquitaine confiscate; initiates first phase of Hundred Years War

1338:   French, Castilian and Genoese galleys roam the Channel virtually unchallenged

1340:   Birth of John of Gaunt; approximate date of birth of Chaucer and **John Hawley**.

1340:   Battle of Sluys

1340:   Five year truce with France begins

1341:   Edward III gifts Dartmouth to Guy de Bryan

1341:   Edward III grants royal charter to the Borough of Clifton-Dartmouth –Hardness

1341:   William Bacon becomes first mayor of Dartmouth

1341:   Claim lodged against Dartmouth privateers operating off coast of Brittany

1343:   Indenture between borough and Guy de Bryan signed by **John Hawley's** father

1344:   **John Hawley's** parents granted land by the Fosse to extend their quay

1344:   Austin Friars ordered to demolish chapel; the visit of 'Brother Hugo'

1345:   Negotiations break down over the Agenais; war recommences

1345:   Dartmouth privateer fleet cruising off Brittany

1346:   Siege of Calais; 31 Dartmouth ships in support

1346:   Spanish ship's master makes claim against William Smale

1349:   Black Death arrives in Dartmouth; probably kills one-third of population

1353:   Ordinance of the Staple enables merchants to seek redress against privateers

1356:   Black Prince captures John II of France at the Battle of Poitiers

1360:   Treaty of Brétigny initiates ten-year truce

1360:   William Smale's privateers attack Flemish vessel, killing 100

1364:   John II dies in captivity in England; Charles V crowned king of France

1365:   War by proxy in Castile

1369:   Alleging breaches of the Treaty of Brétigny, Charles V recommences hostilities.

1372:   First appearance of **John Hawley** in the record – *Le James* arrested for royal service

1372:   Trinity Church (subsequently St Saviour's) consecrated by Bishop Brantyngham

1373:   Geoffrey Chaucer visits Dartmouth; almost certainly meets **John Hawley**

1374-5: **John Hawley** mayor for first time

1376-7: **John Hawley** mayor

1377:   Poll tax record shows **John Hawley** as a prosperous man with four servants

1377:   Edward III dies, Richard II crowned at age of ten.

1377:   Two-year truce ends; Jean de Vienne attacks southern towns, including Dartmouth

1378-9: **John Hawley** mayor

1379:   **Hawley**, Asshenden and de Bottesana obtain letter of marque to attack king's enemies

1381:   Peasants' Revolt

1382-3: **John Hawley** mayor

1384:   **Hawley** and Asshenden sail to Brittany under letters of protection; attacked by Bretons

1385-6: **John Hawley** mayor

1386:   Dartmouth privateers based at St Mathieu

1386:   The *Batel of* **Hawley's** *Barge*

1387:   Jean de Vienne assembles invasion fleet at Harfleur

1387-8: **John Hawley** mayor

1388-9: **John Hawley** mayor

1388:   **Hawley** collector of customs from Melcombe to Bridgwater

1388:   Mayor and burgesses order to construct a *"fortalice by the sea"*

1388:   Merciless Parliament sentences Robert Tresilian to death

1389:   **Hawley** acquires Tresilian estates in Cornwall

1389:   Large wine convoy captured, probably by **Hawley**

1389:   Treaty of Leulingham initiates ten-year truce

1390-1: **John Hawley** mayor

1390:   **Hawley** elected MP for Dartmouth, with Thomas Asshenden

1390:   Dartmouth granted Tin Staple

1392:   Tin Staple moved to Calais

1392-3: **John Hawley** mayor

1393:   Trial of de Roches vs. **Hawley** commences at Westminster

1393:   **Hawley** elected MP for Dartmouth, with John Ellemede

1393-4: **John Hawley** mayor

1394:   **Hawley** elected MP for Dartmouth, with William Damiet

1394:   Joan, first wife of **John Hawley** dies

1394-5: **John Hawley** mayor

1395:   **Hawley** gains armigerous rank, granted by Richard II

1396:   **Hawley's** ships part of flotilla accompanying Richard II to his marriage with Isabella

1397-8: **John Hawley** mayor

1397:   Barbican outpost of Brest relinquished

1398-9: **John Hawley** mayor

1399:   Richard II deposed by Henry Bolingbroke; (Henry IV) dies at Pontefract

1399:   **Hawley**, Spicer et.al. patrol Channel coast

1400-1: **John Hawley** mayor for last time

1402: Franco-Scottish fleet sails from Harfleur; privateers counterattack

1402: Henry IV marries Joan of Navarre

1402: **Hawley** elected MP for Dartmouth for last time, with Ralph North

1402: Hotspur defeats the Scots at Homildon Hill

1403: Du Châtel attacks Plymouth; Wilford expedition in reprisal

1403: Alice, second wife of **John Hawley**, dies

1403: **Hawley** ordered to sea to fight Breton truce-breakers; cruise with Thomas Norton

1404: Hostilities with France formally recommence after Orléans marches on Gascony

1404: Battle of Blackpool

1404: Henry IV expedition to Scotland

1406: Long Parliament discusses abortive plan to licence merchant fleets for sea defence

1406: **John Hawley** incarcerated in Tower of London for two months

1407: Dartmouth privateers running out of control

1407: Duke of Orléans murdered; sparks civil war in France

1408: **John Hawley** dies on December 30th

1410: **John Hawley the younger** elected MP for Dartmouth

1412: **The younger Hawley** involved in fight with the *George of Paignton*

1413: Henry IV dies; Henry V crowned

1414: **John Hawley the younger** elected MP for Dartmouth

1415: Siege of Harfleur; **Hawley the younger** involved in logistics

1415: Battle of Agincourt

1418: Henry V invades Normandy; **Hawley** fails to answer summons; lands confiscated

1419; **Hawley** patrolling east of Cherbourg with Sir Hugh Courtenay

1420: **Hawley** patrolling Channel with personal force of 100 archers and 50 men-at-arms

1420 Treaty of Troyes

1422: Henry V dies; infant Henry VI accedes under regency

1427: Last known capture at sea by a **Hawley** ship

1429: Joan of Arc raises the siege of Orléans; tide of war turns

1436: **John Hawley the younger** dies on May 8th

1449: Wemyngton captures neutral fleet

1452: Henry VI calls upon Dartmouth ships to defend Calais

1453: Aquitaine overrun by French and Hundred Years War effectively ends at Battle of Castillon

Selected Bibliography

Ackroyd, Peter, *Chaucer*, Chatto & Windus, 2004

Alexander, J.J., *Dartmouth as a Parliamentary Borough*, Proceedings of the Devonshire Association, 1911

Allmand, Christopher, *The Hundred Years War; England and France at War c.1300-c.1450*, Cambridge 1989

Bradbury, Jim, *The Medieval Siege*, Boydell, 1992

Carus-Wilson, Eleanora, *Medieval Merchant Venturers*, Methuen, 1954

Chaucer, Geoffrey, *The Canterbury Tales*, the Folio Society, London, 1998

Featherstone, Donald, *The Bowmen of England*, Pen and Sword Military Classics, 1968

Ford, C.J.: *Piracy or Policy: The Crisis in the Channel, 1400-1403*. Transactions of the Royal Historical Society, 5th Ser., Vol. 29, 1979

Freeman, Ray, *Dartmouth and its Neighbours*, Dart Books, 1990/updated Richard Webb 2007

Gardiner, Dorothy A., *John Hawley of Dartmouth*, Transactions of the Devonshire Association, Vol. 98, 1966

Gardiner, Dorothy A., *A Calendar of Early Chancery Proceedings Relating to Westcountry Shipping 1388-1493* Devon & Cornwall Society, 1976

Given-Wilson, C; Brand, P.; Curry, A., Horrox, R.E.; Martin, G., Ormrod, W.M., Phillips, J.R.S., *The Parliamentary Rolls of Medieval England*, The National Archives, 2005 (on CD-ROM)

Harriss, Gerald, *Shaping the Nation; England 1360-1461*, Oxford, 2005

Hoskins, W.G., *Devon*, David & Charles, *1972*

James, Margery K., *A London Merchant in the Fourteenth Century*, *The Economic History Review*, New Series, Vol. 8, No. 3 1956

Jones, Terry, *Chaucer's Knight; the Portrait of a Medieval Mercenary*, Methuen, 1985

Karkeek , Paul Q., *Notes on the Early History of Dartmouth* in Proceedings of the Devonshire Association, read at Totnes, July 1880

Karkeek , Paul Q., *The Shipping and Commerce of Dartmouth in the Reign of Richard II* in Proceedings of the Devonshire Association, read at Dawlish, July 1881

Kowaleski, Maryanne, *The 1377 Dartmouth Poll Tax*, Devon and Cornwall Notes and Queries, Vol. 35, Part 8, 1985

Lewis, Michael, *The History of the British Navy*, Allen & Unwin 1957

Marcus, G.J. *The Naval History of England*, Little Brown, 1961

McKisack, May, *The Fourteenth Century 1307-1399*, Oxford, 1959

Michell Whitley, H., *The Maritime Trade of Exeter in Medieval Times*, Proceedings of the Devonshire Association, 1912

Mortimer, Ian, *The Fears of Henry IV; the Life of England's Self-Made King*, Jonathan Cape, 2007

Mortimer, Ian, *The Perfect King; the Life of Edward III Father of the English Nation*, Pimlico, 2007

Naphy, William and Spicer, Andrew, *The Black Death*, Tempus, 2000

Pearsall, Derek, *The Life of Geoffrey Chaucer*, Blackwell, 1992

Pistono, Stephen, *Henry IV and John Hawley, Privateer, 1399-1408* in Transactions of the Devonshire Association III 1979

Pryor, John H., *Geography, technology and war; studies in the maritime history of the Mediterranean 649-1571*, Cambridge 1992

Rodger, Nicholas A.M., *The Safeguard of the Sea; A Naval History of Britain, 660-1649*, Penguin, 2004

Rose, Susan, *Medieval Naval Warfare 1000-1500*, Routledge, 2002

Roskell, J.S, Clarke, Linda & Rawcliffe, Carole, *The House of Commons 1386 -1421*, the History of Parliament Trust, 1992

Russell, Percy, *Dartmouth*, Friends of the Dartmouth Museum Association, 1950

Stanes, R.G.F., *Sir Guy de Bryan K.G.*, Transactions of the Devonshire Association, 1959

Stonor Saunders, Frances, *Hawkwood – Diabolical Englishman*, Faber, 2004

Unger, Richard W., *The Ship in the Medieval Economy 600-1600*, Croom Helm, 1980

Unwin, Peter, *The Narrow Sea*, Review, 2003

Various authors, *Oxford Dictionary of National Biography* (online version)

Wadge, Richard, *Arrowstorm; the World of the Archer in the Hundred Years War*, Spellmount, 2007

Watkin, Hugh R., *Dartmouth Pre-Reformation*, the Devonshire Association, 1935

White, Florence E., *Chaucer's Shipman*, in *Modern Philology*,1928-9, vol.26

Windeatt, Edward, *The Borough of Clifton-Dartmouth- Hardness and its Mayors and Mayoralties*. Proceedings of the Devonshire Association, 1911

Ziegler, Philip, *The Black Death*, Harper Collins, 1969

Endnotes

1   Freeman, Ray, Dartmouth and its Neighbours, 2007, p.11

2   Watkin, Hugh R., "Dartmouth pre-Reformation" Parochial Histories of Devonshire no. 5; The Devonshire Association, 1935, p.16

3   ibid. p.17

4   Watkin, p.353

5   Calendar of Patent Rolls Henry III, vol.5, p.421(online access courtesy of the University of Iowa)

6   Watkin, p.9

7   Ibid. p.14

8   CPR Henry III, vol 6, p.432

9   Watkin, pp.38-41

10   CPR Edward III, vol.6, p.48

11   Watkin, passim

12   CPR Richard II, vol.4, p.253

13   For a fuller account of this and the history of the other Dartmouth churches, see Freeman, op.cit. passim

14   James, Margery K. A London Merchant of the Fourteenth Century in The Economic History Review, New Series, Vol. 8, No. 3, 1956, pp. 364-376

15   Hoskins, W.G., Devon 1954, p.59

16   Watkin, p.44

17   Ziegler, Philip, The Black Death, 1969 p.136

18   Watkin, op.cit., p.49

19   Ibid. pp.48-9

20   Watkin, p.79

21   The brave reader may which to consult, for example, A.R.Bridbury, "The Black Death" in the Economic History Review, New Series, Vol.26, no. 4. 1973

22   European State Finance Database Project: http://www.le.ac.uk/hi/bon/ESFDB/MMB/einm001.txt

23   Karkeek, Paul Q., The Shipping and Commerce of Dartmouth in the Reign of Richard II in the Proceedings of the Devonshire Association, July 1881, pp.189-90

24   James, Margery K., The Fluctuations of the Anglogascon Wine Trade during the Fourteenth Century; in Economic History Review, New Series, Vol. 4 no.2 p.176

25   Ibid. p.182

26   Runyan, Timothy J., Ships and Fleets in Anglo-French Warfare 1337-1360, in American Neptune, vol.46, 1986

27   CPR Henry VI, vol.6, p.244

28   Unger, Richard W., The Ship in the Medieval Economy 600-1400, p.163

29   Rose, Susan, Medieval Naval Warfare 1000-1500, p.59.

30   Rodger, N.A.M., The Safeguard of the Sea; A Naval History of Britain, 660-1649, p.96

31   Rodger, op.cit. p.118

32   CPR Henry III, vol. 4, p.363

33   Rodger, op.cit. p.119

34   Rodger, op.cit. p. 121, citing Gardiner "Westcountry Shipping"

35   Rose, op.cit. p.20

36   ibid. p.119

37   Runyan, op.cit.

38   Watkin, p.58

39   Ibid.

40   CPR, Edward III, vol.5, p.210

41   CPR, Edward III, vol.7, p.100

42   ibid.

43   CPR, Edward III, vol.11, p.585

44   CPR, Edward III, vol.12, p.492

45   CPR, Edward III, vol.14, p.133

46   ibid. p.73

47   Karkeek, P., Shipping in 14th Century Dartmouth in Transactions of the Devonshire Association, 1880-81, p.585

48   Watkin, p.59

49   CPR, Edward III, vol.16, p.32

50   Roskell, J.S, Clarke, Linda & Rawcliffe, Carole, The House of Commons 1386 -1421, vol. II, p.74

51   CPR, Richard II, vol. 1, p.356

52   CPR, Richard II, vol. 1, p.405

53   Gardiner, op.cit. pp.177-8

54   A detailed description of the proceedings, on which this account is based, is given by Florence E. White in Chaucer's Shipman, in three instalments in Modern Philology,1928-9, vol.26 no.2 pp.249-55;vol. 27 No.1. pp.123-8; vol.27 p.123-

55   White, op.cit. (conclusion), p.127

56   Roskell et.al. op.cit. vol. IV, p.218

57   CPR, Henry IV, vol. 4, p.65

58   CPR, Richard II, vol. 3, p.165

59   Ibid. p.372

60   Nicolas, Nicholas, A History of the Royal Navy, Vol. II, p.329

61   Gardiner, op.cit. pp188-9

62   CPR, Richard II, vol. 3, p.500

63   Ibid.

64   Ibid. p.426

65   Russell, op.cit. p.40

66   CPR, Richard II, vol.3, p.499
67   CPR, Richard II, vol.4, p.338
68   Calendar of Parliament Rolls, November 3rd 1391, iii, pp-295-6
69   Ibid.
70   Leland, John L. Oxford Dictionary of National Biography (online version)
71   CPR, Richard II, vol. 4, p.156
72   Watkin, p.371
73   Ibid.
74   CPR, Richard II, vol.4, p.359
75   CPR, Henry IV, vol.2, p.108
76   Roskell et.al. op.cit. vol II, pp59-9
77   Ibid. vol III, p.330
78   CPR, Richard II, vol.4, p.390
79   Calendar of Parliament Rolls, 1393, iii, pp.300-1
80   CPR, Henry IV, vol.2, p.198
81   Ibid. p.195
82   Ibid. p.198
83   For an excellent, detailed analysis of this question, and of the "pirate war" in general, see: Ford, C.J.: Piracy or Policy: The Crisis in the Channel, 1400-1403. Transactions of the Royal Historical Society, 5th Ser., Vol. 29, 1979, pp. 63-78.
84   CPR, Henry IV, vol.2, p.356
85   Ibid. p.363
86   Ibid. p.428
87   For Percy Russell's interpretation of the battle see: Russell, op.cit. pp. 42-47
88   Nicolas, op.cit. p. 363
89   Quoted in a footnote in Nicolas, op.cit. p.365
90   CPR, Henry IV, vol.2, p.430
91   Ibid. p.310

92   Russell, op.cit. pp. 46-7
93   CPR, Henry IV, vol.2, p.430
94   CPR, Henry IV, vol.3, p.152
95   CPR Henry IV vol.2, p.425
96   Pistono, Stephen, Henry IV and John Hawley, Privateer, 1399-1408 in Transactions of the Devonshire Association III 1979 pp.145-163
97   Calendar of Parliament Rolls 1406 iii p.570
98   Gardiner, op.cit. p.201
99   CPR, Henry IV, vol.1, p.404
100 CPR, Henry IV, vol.2, p.360
101 Ibid. p.437
102 CPR, Henry IV, vol.3, p.245
103 CPR, Henry IV, vol.4, p.316
104 Ibid. p.381
105 Gardiner, Dorothy A., A Calendar of Early Chancery Proceedings Relating to Westcountry Shipping 1388-1493, pp.15-16
106 CPR, Henry V, vol.1, p.36
107 Ibid. P.35
108 Ibid.
109 Ibid. p.116
110 Ibid. p.256
111 Ibid. p.348
112 Roskell et.al. op.cit. vol.III, p.331
113 CPR, Henry V, vol.2, p.274
114 CPR, Henry VI vol.2, p.301
115 Watkin, p.298
116 Op.cit p.232.
117 Galway, op.cit. p.501
118 Ibid.
119 Karkeek, Paul Q., Notes on the Early History of Dartmouth in Transactions of the Devonshire Association, read at Totnes, July 1880, p.586
120 Freeman, op.cit. p.33

Index

Numbers in bold refer to pages on which illustrations of the subject appear.

Disclaimer

The author and publisher have made every effort to find and correctly attribute the copyright of material that is not already in the public domain but if they have inadvertently used or credited any material inappropriately, please could the copyright holder contact the author or the publisher so that a full credit can be given in the next edition.